SOCIAL

CAPITALISM

A return to balance and reason

By: Lawrence F. Mignogna

In loving memory of my father
Raymond F. Mignogna PhD.
Who throughout life as an engineer and educator
Often expressed a desire to go into economics.
This one's for you Dad

CONTENTS

Chapter 5- Economies Unbalanced

Part III
Yesterday, Today and Tomorrow

Chapter 6- Taxes and Their Effects

Chapter 7- Current Problems and Arguments

Chapter 8- What We Need to Do

Chapter 9- Our Government At Work

PROLOGUE

I would like to start by saying, "Thank you" to you all for taking the time to pick up this book. I hope you enjoy reading it. My intentions are not to stir up controversy or anger. It seems we already have enough anger and resentments in this world.

In today's America we have an ever-growing divide between people's philosophies concerning how our country should be run. Our elected leaders are stuck in gridlock due to extreme partisan views, making positive, workable solutions almost impossible.   Especially in these trying economic times with high unemployment, the people of today need progress from our government, but it seems that little to nothing positive is getting done.   We have economic issues that involve: high unemployment, sluggish business growth, expanding debts, and unfair tax codes, just to name a few. There are other issues such as immigration and education, which can also impact our economy. The constant bickering and gridlock makes finding solutions to these problems almost impossible.

There are those on the far left and right who support only the extreme form of their ideology.   On one side we have the extreme Republicans who believe in the need to practice pure capitalism in its extreme form. On the other side are extreme Liberals who pursue expanded socialist styles of government.   I believe that the views of most Americans lay more towards the center of the spectrum. It is the politicians and pundits who lead us to think Americans are just as partisan as the leaders we've elected. It is my intent to try and bring us together, to realize that we are all Americans with the same goals. However, our political problems arise because we have very different views of how to achieve these goals.

I am not a trained economist (but neither was any president). Nor am I a politician, but more a concerned citizen. In this book I would like to share with you some of my own educated opinions and ideas based on some of my own research as well as the findings of others. I do not wish to preach, nor intend for my words to be considered gospel and accepted by all. What I hope to accomplish in this book is to spark debate and new ideas in a civil, moderate fashion backed by intelligent reasoning.

When I say intelligent reasoning, I am referring in contrast to the style of debating used by most politicians and pundits of today; arguments that use extreme generalizations and narrow or incomplete facts to discuss complex situations. Just turn on the TV to a news talk show. If the host is interviewing a politician or commentator with a little (R) or (D) next to their name, can you guess what words are going to come out of their mouths next? You and many other Americans probably can. Simplicity used in debates on today's TV news shows is not the complete the fault of our politicians. In today's sound-byte driven media with strict time frames, the use of quick talking points and generalizations are required. This book is intended to be a more in-depth discussion concerning the issues of today, which many of us only hear and understand from the quick talking points we see on TV.

It is my belief that our best economic times occurred when we have worked together, taking a moderate stance finding balance between the ideas of the far right and left. In this book I will show you how and when these periods of balance and growth occurred. I also believe we faced our most trying times when economic policy strayed too far from the center, too far to the left or right upsetting our balance of ideas. We will go through some of the issues facing our nation today trying to reason through and find a balanced approach to solving our problems. I hope to strike this balance by focusing on our common goals, understanding the different beliefs behind our ideologies, and by using research based on historical facts that shows what has and has not worked in the past.

In order to advance the discussion in a thoughtful manner, this book is divided into three parts. The first part of the book sets the stage for us and provides a basis for our discussion. Part II, titled, "Finding Balance" uses theoretical reasoning to strike a consensus among differing views points. Finally in Part III, we dive into the specific problems of today; discussing topics such as tax policy, the economy, Social Security and our national debt. We hope to find solutions to these problems by applying a balanced approach of reasoning and thinking.

If my words are convincing enough to some people, then great. But if not, at least I hope this book can help give another perspective and show a new way to think through some of the issues of today.

After reading I invite you all to post further comments, questions, ideas, or criticisms to my webpage at www.socialcapitalismonline.com/ Please keep it civil and thoughtful. Remember we are all in this together as one nation. If we the people can first come to a moderate consensus, maybe we can demand the same of our politicians. Then finally we can get something accomplished that benefits our entire nation and all our citizens.

Part 1
Our Great Nation
and
Who We Are

Chapter 1

The Purpose of Government

The Birth of a Nation; Our Founding Father's Intentions

"We the People of the United States, in Order to form a more perfect Union, establish Justice, insure domestic Tranquility, provide for the common defense, promote the General Welfare, and secure the Blessings of Liberty to ourselves and our Posterity, do Ordain and establish this Constitution for the United States of America."
-Constitution of the United States of America ₁

This is the preamble to the U.S. Constitution. What exactly does that mean? Preamble? A preamble is a statement that explains the intent or purpose for a document that is to follow. These words in the preamble to the Constitution are our forefather's intent. It is what they hoped to accomplish and achieve by writing the Constitution.

All the articles of the Constitution following the preamble are an outline for government. It is a set of laws that were written in the hope of accomplishing the goals written in the preamble. Many articles may not be perfect and there were still many issues not addressed in the Constitution, especially issues that were unforeseen at the time. Many aspects concerning today's modern society were not specifically addressed in the Constitution. For the following two hundred years since it was first written, we have been adding and changing particular laws and rules, all in the hope of better achieving those goals laid out in the preamble to the Constitution.

Before continuing to read this book, please again look above and read the preamble to our Constitution. Look at each line carefully and ask yourself: Do you agree with what is written? As you read each line carefully, create your own understanding of what the words mean to you. Do you want to form a more perfect Union? Do you want to insure domestic Tranquility, promote the General Welfare, and secure the blessings of Liberty?

15

Our story as a country should reflect the story of our people. Our democratic government was setup by the people and therefore our government is intended to function for the people. From the start of its conception, we have been debating how our government can best serve the people of our nation.

In trying to achieve these goals laid out in the preamble we are guided by today's set of moral principles and beliefs. Beliefs such as: we are all created equal; that we all have a right to life, liberty and the pursuit of happiness; all form the basis of how we should reach our goals. In order to help govern ourselves with these principles in mind, the Constitution of the United States was written. After much debate and scrutiny our Constitution has so far withstood the test of time. Over two hundred years later most (if not all Americans) still believe and cherish this document. We view the Constitution as a document that reflects our morals and should be used as a guide to ensure all of our rights and liberties. Our love for country and the core principles expressed in the preamble is probably why so many people and politicians use quotes from this document all the time.

So how do we form a more perfect union, establish justice, insure domestic tranquility, promote the general welfare and secure the blessings of liberty to ourselves and our posterity? Our founding fathers started by outlining the specific rules to establish a democratic government for the people. But much that pertains to our daily lives today was left out to interpret ourselves. One of the biggest factors affecting the life of all citizens is that of the economy and our economic system.

Unfortunately there is no guide, bible or magic book that was handed to us telling how we should handle our economy. Aside from a few rules regarding taxation, nowhere in the Constitution does it say plainly what economic policies we should adhere to or enact. We look to the Constitution as a guide, to interpret it and see how we should handle economic matters. Much like religious scholars try interpreting the Bible to see, "What would Jesus do?" regarding a particular aspect of modern life that didn't exist two thousand years ago, we too look towards the Constitution to see how we should handle economic matters in a global world that was unforeseen long ago in the 1700s.

If we read the preamble to the Constitution it contains the phrases "perfect UNION" and "general WELFARE". Wow! These sound like words and terms used to describe socialism! What about the term "COMMON defense"? The word "common" is also often associated with socialism. But what about "Freedom" and "Free markets"?

It wasn't until The Bill of Rights was added to the Constitution in 1791, that we see the word "freedom". Freedom isn't mentioned in the Constitution at all, not once! Not until the amendments were added did the word "freedom" become associated with the Constitution.

So now we have two ideas from the Constitution: we have <u>Freedom</u> and we have the <u>General Welfare</u>. When thinking how these words should pertain to our economic system, from the word "freedom" we interpret it to mean "free market" or as it's also called, "capitalism"; the freedom to make money (or not make money if you freely choose to be lazy).

The government is supposed to protect and ensure our right to freedom, which people assume includes the freedom to make money. We should all be free to be the best we can; having the freedom to work hard and in turn for it to be profitable for us. We have the right to pursue our dreams, provide for our families and strive to become more than what we are. This is the American Dream; an idea that has been with us for years and the envy of the world. It's an idea that so many other people strive for. This is why we have formed and expanded our ideas of capitalism as a way for our people to prosper under the guidelines of the Constitution.

But the government according to the Constitution is also supposed to promote the general welfare and ensure liberty to the people. Unfortunately, we find many instances where the general welfare and people's liberties are often in conflict with the theories and outcomes of capitalism and free markets. These conflicts of interests will be an ongoing theme we will continue to analyze throughout this book.

Then there are the ideas and theories of socialism, where the government controls aspects of the economy in the hope of ensuring the general welfare for the people.

Government controlling the means of production and policies that place controls or regulations on private industries are all aspects of socialist ideals. Socialism promotes using tax dollars for certain social programs or social needs, which capitalists argue should be handled by private industry.

I do not wish to support one theory over the other. As with everything, there is good and bad inherent in any and every system. What I wish to strive for is the intentions of our forefathers, that which is written in our Constitution that we all cherish. After analyzing both theories in the best interests of our country's citizens, I hope to pick out the best from both theories and combine them into one, which I call Social Capitalism.

Actually, we already have a system that could be called "Social Capitalism", utilizing ideas from both socialism and capitalism. We have free market practices which reward hard work and ambition. We also have many social practices such as public schools, public roads and defense all in the interest of promoting the general welfare. So far this system in the U.S. has been predominately called a "mixed economy", meaning that we incorporate both social and capitalistic ideas.

I am not writing this so that BP Oil should be allowed to ignore safety concerns, nor am I writing this so that the lazy bum, who turned into an alcoholic, can collect another welfare check from hard working taxpayers. I am writing this so we as a country can continue to discuss how to best ensure our freedoms while at the same time ensure the basic welfare and liberty for all.

Things may not be perfect, but many can agree we have it better than most people in other countries. Of course there is still a lot of work to be done, changing this law or abolishing that one. We pride ourselves on being the best nation in the world. The main reason for our success is because we have utilized the best parts from the theories of capitalism and socialism. Even though we may be the most powerful nation, we are far from perfect and have our share of big problems. But I do not believe that extremism is the answer to solving our issues. We cannot solve all of our problems by adhering to only one theory over the other. We have always taken the best of the best from both schools of thought.

Extremist thinkers of today label capitalism and socialism as that of good or bad. People have come up with positive and negative connotations for both theories. Unfortunately, the extreme ideas behind socialism and capitalism have become the basis for which many label our political parties. Republicans are considered to be capitalists and Democrats are thought to be socialists. This is how the political parties have been portrayed recently in the media. Bill O'Reilly and Sean Hannity on Fox News constantly refer to the policies of the Obama administration as those of a socialist regime. Then you have Chris Matthews of MSNBC referring to the Republicans as supporters of extreme capitalism and the corporate greed that can ensue from it. People easily categorize and assume you are either one or the other. "You are with us or against us", has been the thinking of so many extremist politicians who force voters to choose one extreme or the other.

What I hope to accomplish here is to show that there is a middle way. These things don't have to be so black and white. There is a grey area, which most American's beliefs fall under. A 2009 Gallup poll conducted shows that 42% of Americans call themselves Moderate, a Liberal Republican or a Conservative Democrat. An additional 17% call themselves Moderate Republicans or Moderate Democrats.[ii] These people all believe in some form of balance between ideas; and that is Social Capitalism. We cannot let the extremist of either party sway our voices or our votes to support one extreme theory over the other. There is a middle way.

Role of Government: Big or Small?

There has always been debate considering the size of our government, its budget and how far its reach can affect the markets and our personal lives. Should we have big government or small government? Should there be high taxes with vast social programs or should there be lower taxes, leaving certain needs and services to be provided by private industry and the free market. Extreme capitalists argue for smaller government, allowing private industry to handle all needs and services. Extreme socialists argue for bigger government, thinking that private businesses cannot be counted on to provide certain services and needs for the people.

I say the size of the government shouldn't be too big or too small. The size of the government should be the perfect size, in a perfect world. That ideal size of government can be dictated by one simple principle:

-The size and reach of the government should be determined by what it is mandated to accomplish.

According to our constitution the government is mandated to protect the freedoms and liberty of every individual. The Constitution also mandates that it is the responsibility of the government to ensure the welfare of the public, which is written clearly in the preamble that no American should be able to argue with.

So, we are all supposed to be free. The government of the U.S. is set up to ensure our freedoms; to provide an environment in which we are all free to do as we choose. We are all free to practice whatever religion and say what we want to say. We are free to choose this job or that job. We are free to buy this product or that one. The basis of this country, the thing that makes America great is our freedoms. Under these "freedoms" we have the free market or our capitalistic system. We are free to work and free to earn money.

But the government is also charged with the responsibility to ensure the "General Welfare" of society as a whole. The government accomplishes this by providing security through our military, police and firefighters. Other aspects that promote the general welfare can be seen in the protecting of property rights, the set up and maintenance of needed infrastructure and institutions such as the Departments of Health, Labor, Commerce, etc.

So how big or small should our government be? The answer is: Big enough to be able to carry out it's mandated purpose as laid out in the Constitution and no bigger.

How Free Are We?

We say that we are a free society. We are free to do anything, right? Absolutely Not! Yes we are a free society, more than any other country or system. Does that mean we should be completely free to do as we choose at anytime concerning any aspect of our lives? Or is there a limit to our freedom? We are not completely free to do as we please 100% unconditionally. But people loosely throw around the word freedom as if we are or should be 100% free. Where do our freedoms stop? Where or how do you limit freedom in a free society? Here is another principle that should be reflected in any society that is to promote freedom and the general welfare at the same time.

-*Your freedoms in a free society are limited to anything that doesn't infringe on the freedoms or well being of other people.*

-*You are free up to the point at which you start to infringe on the freedoms of others.*

These are simple ideas I think few would disagree with. We are free to do as we please as long as it doesn't affect the freedoms or well being of others in society. Here is another example of where there is a delicate balance that needs to be reached. The government needs to both protect the individual freedoms of people as well as ensure the welfare of its people. Policies or laws that grant or favor the concepts of freedom in the marketplace could infringe upon the freedoms and well being of other people. In the converse, too much attention or priority given to the well being of society as a whole can limit or encroach upon the freedoms of individuals.

And so we go back to the question concerning the size of government. Should government be big or small? The answer according to Social Capitalism is that it shouldn't be too big that it has over reaching powers and limits people's freedoms, nor should it be too small where it allows certain people to do whatever they want, negatively effecting other people's rights, freedoms or well being.

We need to balance the idea of individual freedom

21

with the idea of public welfare. This balance cannot be reached if there are extremist on both sides who try and persuade us with general thoughts; saying we need smaller government or bigger government. Government shouldn't be either big or small. It should be just right.

Balanced Market Economy?

What does it mean to have a "balanced market"? What determines if the economy is doing well or not? Normally we look at Gross Domestic Product (GDP) and Gross Domestic Income (GDI) to determine the health of the economy. But looking at these figures alone does not give a full perspective and can be misleading. Suppose GDP numbers have risen, but only 1% of the population earns all the money and the other 99% of people live in poverty. Is this a sign of a healthy economy? What about unemployment rates? If there is a low unemployment rate of .01%, but most of the jobs are low paying, is this a sign of a healthy economy? Any country's strongest economic times are when a majority of the people can live within a range close to the average income and average standard of living. There are a few people who live better and a few worse, but the majority is able to live decent lives. This is the middle class. The truest sign of a country with a healthy, balanced economy is one where its GDP grows at the same rate as the average person's income. This doesn't mean that individuals can't rise above or fall below the average. As long as most people are able to live productive, healthy lives, earning a decent living, then you could say we have a healthy economy. The more people do better, the better our country is doing as a whole. However, if a majority of people slips below the average, then we could say that the market is not balanced and the economy is not healthy.

Shouldn't it be the position of our government in order to accomplish its purpose of promoting the general welfare, pass economic policies that attempt to benefit the greatest amount of people in society as a whole? Some believe policies that only promote capitalistic ideals are the best way to ensure the welfare of our country. Then there are those who believe more socialist leaning policies best ensure the welfare of the people.

What policies best promote the prosperity of our country? To reach our goal of obtaining a "balanced market" what policies will allow most of our citizens to flourish? To answer this we first must use a comprehensive approach towards judging the prosperity of our economy. We cannot look only at numbers of GDP or unemployment. We must look at the overall economic picture.

There are systems and indexes in use that look at other aspects of our economy. One of the most important reflections of a balanced, healthy economy is the Gini Index, which measures income inequality. The Italian statistician Corrado Gini developed the Gini index in 1912. It is this index that has been used by economists around the world to show wealth disparity. The Gini index uses a ratio from 0-1. Numbers closer to zero represent an equal income distribution throughout the population. Numbers closer to 1 represent a huge difference in income, which translates to a larger gap between the rich and poor.

The chart below shows Gini Index numbers for some countries around the world in 2009. The United States, China, most of South America, and many parts of Africa all have higher income disparities between rich and poor. [iii]

Gini Coefficients Worldwide

< .60	South Africa, Zimbabwe, Botswana, Namibia
.55-.59	Columbia, Bolivia, Panama
.50-.54	Brazil, Peru, Chile, Niger, Zambia
.45-.49	U.S.A. China, Argentina, Mozambique, Venezuela
.40-.44	Russia, Turkey, Iran, Thailand
.35-.39	India, Japan, Indonesia, Portugal, Algeria
.30-.34	Australia, Canada, England, France, Italy, Switzerland
.25-.29	Germany, Norway, Austria, Belgium
> .25	Sweden

Source: CIA World Factbook 2009

23

Nations with the smallest Gini Indexes are all countries in Europe, Canada, Australia, and most of Asia. The distribution of wealth in America is on par and comparable to some of the poorest nations in the world. China, which is considered a communist country, has actually become the largest free market country in the world. Yes, it is still controlled by an aristocracy, but it has taken on free market ideals with little to no government regulation over private business. While its economy has grown significantly, China also has had a 30% increase in the income gap between rich and poor over the past twenty years.[iv] While many would still call China a communist country, its actual policies over the past twenty years have been more like that of strict free market capitalism.

Milton Friedman was one of the most influential economists during the second half of the 20th Century, who headed the Chicago School of Economics. He supported strict capitalistic theory and government deregulation, serving as economic advisor to President Reagan in the 1980s. During the 70s and 80s, Friedman and others from his Chicago School also served as economic advisors to most of the South American dictatorships. These dictatorships were able to impose Freidman's strict ideals of capitalism unlike any democracy could ever do. One result of these experiments in "pure capitalism" turned out to be a substantial expansion in the gap between rich and poor throughout South America.[v]

During the 1940s, 50s, and 60s the United States has had a lower Gini Index number compared to our European counter-parts. But over the past 30 years, starting in the 1970s, the gap between rich and poor has been rising exponentially along with the further free market policies we have enacted.

As a democracy with a government for the people by the people, shouldn't we try and achieve a balanced economy; an economy where a majority of our citizens are able to live around the average income, reflected by a Gini Index number that is closer to 0? A growing gap between rich and poor is not a sign of a healthy, balanced economy. Shouldn't this gap between rich and poor be lessened as much as possible without encroaching upon the individual freedoms of our people?

Shouldn't this be one of the most important reflections of a balanced market and healthy economy our government should strive to achieve?

Chapter 2

Who We Are

Despite our differences we are all the same.

My main goal is not to fuel further resentment amongst liberals and conservatives. Even though many of us differ in our ideas and thinking, remember that we are all Americans with a common purpose. In order to work together, to find solutions for our problems, we must first establish our common goals. Conservatives and liberals don't differ because of opposing goals. We have political division because we disagree on the methods that should be used to achieve our common goals.

To start we should try and find those things that all Americans (and I would like to invite the rest of the world as well) can agree upon. We are all human beings with the same needs. The most fundamental necessities for all humans are food, shelter and clothing. Societies cannot be stable or safe if a large number of people do not have these basic needs. It is during times of mass poverty that we see uprisings and revolts over and over again around the world. The French Revolution that occurred in the late 18th century is one example. A large portion of the French population was poor and suffering from malnutrition, leading to discontent, revolt and uprising. It is also believed that the recent uprisings in the Middle East were caused by the results of income inequality.[vi] The bottom line is that when people are able to feed themselves and live healthy lives, they are not starting revolts.

Fortunately we have not had huge problems recently with large revolts and uprisings in the U.S. But keep in mind there are many in our country that do not have the basic necessities. Chances are if you bought and are reading this book, this doesn't include you. However it is good to remember that all of our personal situations can change at any moment.

Now that I hope we agree on these basic needs for humanity, we can talk about some other common goals and needs. I would like to continue our discussion of "goals" with those that are laid out beautifully in the preamble to our constitution: Tranquility; Justice; Defense (safety); Liberty for ourselves and our Posterity (our sons and daughters). We all want to live a life of tranquility and liberty. We all want justice and wish to live in a safe place, free of fear for our safety. These goals listed in the preamble are some of our most basic desires, which we can all agree upon as Americans. It is these statements written by our forefathers that make America the envy of the world. Every human on earth shares and hopes to achieve these goals in their own lives.

Next we can list other common goals on a more specific level. This is just a short list of ones that I've come up with. Please place check marks next to each goal I've listed if you agree. I am willing to bet that everyone who reads this list, no matter if you are Republican, Democrat, Liberal, Conservative, White, Black, Buddhist or Christian, will all agree with the following broad statements.

-We should all be free to live our lives.
-Hard work should be rewarded.
-Laziness should not be rewarded.
-We should encourage innovation.
-Everybody who wants a job should be able to have one.
-Everyone who wants an education should have one.
-An educated society is necessary to spur development.
-People who would do ill to others should be punished.
-We don't want to wrongly punish those that have done no wrong.
-Being part of society carries certain responsibilities.
-We don't want to waste our time, effort, or money.
-We all want to live in peace and security, free of fear for our safety.
-All should have an equal opportunity to achieve their dreams.

Maybe you can think of some more general goals or ideas that we can all agree upon.

Now that we have established some common goals I hope we can agree on, let us progress into understanding the harder part; the part where we begin to disagree; the HOW. How do we go about achieving these common goals?

How do we ensure liberty for all? How do we make sure people have their basic needs met? How do we reward hard work? How do we fulfill our responsibilities towards society? How do we not waste time and money? How do we ensure equal opportunity and not just grant equal outcomes?

In Part III we will look further into the methods used to achieve these specific goals. For now, just understand that most of the time it is not the end goals we disagree with, but more the ideas of how do we achieve these goals. Before discussing the "how?" we need to ask "why?" Why do we have different views of how to best achieve our common goals? In the next section we will start to look at why and where we start to form different opinions.

Geographical influenced Beliefs

When looking at a U.S. political map showing red states and blue states it is not hard to see a drastic geographical pattern where people are divided into political parties. (Sorry, but to keep printing costs low the image below is in black and white. The darker areas represent heavily Democratic populations and lighter shades are predominately Republican).

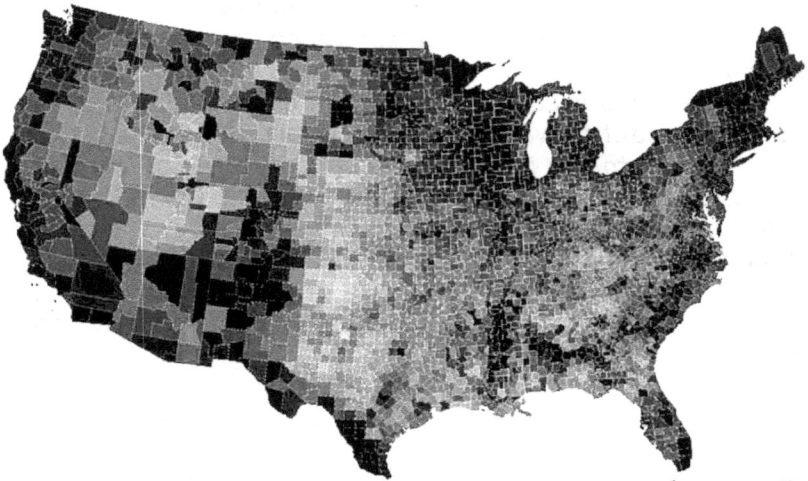

Diagram by: Mark Newman University of Michigan[vii]

Typically people in more urban, highly populated areas tend to be Democrats, with heavy concentrations along the coastal areas and other metropolises. Rural areas tend to be more Republican. Even a heavily red Republican state like Tennessee is dominantly Democratic in its urban cities of Nashville and Memphis.

Why are people from rural America more likely to identify with Republicans and people from higher populated areas more likely to be Democrat? Let's start by coming up with a frame describing each of the political parties.

Republicans are the party of INDIVIDUAL FREEDOM and smaller government as can be seen in their advocacy for policies that limit government, leaving individuals to decide their own destinies. Democrats however tend to be the party of SOCIAL RESPONSIBILITY, where they emphasize a more proactive government working as a force for the collective good.

Why does someone from rural America place more value on "Individual Freedom" and someone from the city place more value on "Social Responsibility"? The answer is quite simple. All you need to do is slip into the mind of a typical rural American and look around at what they see. The average rural American wakes up, looks out their window and may see a large field. You may see no one or very few people for miles. There's lots of space, with no one to bother them and no one for them to bother. If someone grows up in this environment where there is little contact with people, they tend to think; "I can do whatever I want. Nothing I do affects anyone else. There is no one to help me and there is no one for me to help. My land is my land and I can do what I want with it. Whatever I do doesn't affect anyone. If I want to dig a well, I can dig a well. If I want to fish in the creek, I'll fish in the creek." It is easy to see how someone growing up in this situation would question anyone who tried to tell them, especially the government, what they could or couldn't do; what they should or shouldn't do.

On the other side you have people who grow up in more urban settings where they come into contact with thousands of people a day; where they are sharing roads, sidewalks, buses, and subways with thousands of people.

These people can have neighbors literally six inches away, the thickness of an apartment wall. When growing up in this environment, no longer are you raised with a large sense of individual freedom. Growing up in the city you stand in line to wait your turn, you can't blast your radio in the apartment, which could disturb the neighbors. If you throw your trash on the ground and all the other millions of people in Manhattan did the same thing, the place would literally turn into a garbage dump. Millions of workers rely on public transportation to get them to and from work. Mass transit used by the collective is required in big cities. If everyone drove their own car into Manhattan or London it would be physically impossible to place all the cars. We can see how growing up in more urban areas would ingrain in the minds of urbanites a higher sense of social responsibility and the need to work together as part of a larger group.

None of these situations, philosophies or values is wrong. Nor should one take precedent over the other. Individual freedom and social responsibility are both important core values, which were recognized by our founders. The main point here is to be able to put yourself in the other person's shoes, to try and understand where they are coming from. Reasonable, workable agreements that strike a balance, benefiting all people will never be reached without a bit of empathy and understanding on all our parts.

It is because of these differing geographically based views, which is why many aspects of government responsibility tend to be handled and given to the individual states or local governments to deal with. Things like schools systems, alcohol and firearms, and intrastate commerce policies, are mostly governed from the state and local levels of government. There is still ongoing debate as to what issues should be handled at the federal level and what issues should be left up to the states, which is a discussion we will save for another time. Here I would like to keep the focus on the overall responsibility of government as a whole, federal, state and local.

Part II
Finding Balance

Chapter 3
Applying Balance

Yin and Yang: Fighting Extremist thought.

Balance is all around us. Nature as we know it functions because of balance, just as the particles within an atom are held together by the balance of positive and negatively charged particles. Take a moment to look around yourself and think of other aspects in life where you can see the positive effects of balance or duality: give and take; the Yin and Yang; the need to eat a balanced diet and the scales of justice. Just the same, our founding fathers recognized the need for balance in a democracy and formed a government with three branches: the Legislative (Congress); the Executive (the Presidency); and the Judicial (the court system). This government design, with three branches has become known as the "system of checks and balances". With the idea of checks and balances, power was divided over the three branches and certain checks were put into place so that one branch could not hold more power over the others.

Our American system of government is unique in using these ideas of balance and we have extended the use of balance even further. "The rule of the majority while protecting the rights of the minority" is another idea of balance incorporated into our government system. This is why many actions in Congress require 2/3rds approval instead of the typical assumption that a 51% majority wins. These ideas and rules were utilized by our founding fathers to help ensure balance. One could even say that the idea of "innocent till proven guilty" incorporates principles of balance. The concept of "innocent till proven guilty" weighs the treatment and rights of those only suspected of criminal activity who may indeed be innocent, with the rights of known criminals.

If we can so successfully form a government system that has functioned well for over two hundred years, can't we use the same principles of balance to make a successful economic system? I believe we have! In comparison to the rest of the world we have had a very successful economic history. We didn't become the wealthiest, most powerful nation in the world without having a good balanced economic system. How would we define that economic system which has enabled the U.S. to become the most powerful and prosperous nation on earth? Many of us grew up and were taught in school that we have a capitalist system. But we do not have a true capitalistic system and never have! Pure capitalism is free of all government intervention. But the reality is that the United States has never had a true capitalistic system. We have had a mixed economy, balancing ideas from both socialist and capitalist theory. Anything publicly owned is a socialist practice. We have the post office, police departments, public schools, Social Security, fire departments, public utilities, public roads and a whole lot more.

We've been operating since our independence as a mixed economy, which I like to call Social Capitalism. During our entire history we have applied to our economy a balance of ideas that has made us the most powerful nation on earth so far. We have incorporated both socialistic and capitalistic views. Of course we have had our ups and downs. The market goes up, the market goes down. Unemployment is up or down. Things will fluctuate slightly. Sometimes our government will pass this law or that law, which may incorporate more right leaning views or left leaning views. But why have there been occasions where there were drastic market slumps or high unemployment rates? In the chapters that follow I will show that major economic slumps have occurred when we apply too much of one theory, upsetting the balance. When the balance of ideas is no longer maintained allowing extremist thought to lead us too far down one path or the other, our economy takes a turn for the worse. In the following chapters we will talk about the pros and cons of both capitalism and socialistic ideas. We will look at the positive aspects of each theory. By utilizing the good from both in order to maintain a balanced system, we can avoid the problems that may arise if we stray to far from the middle.

Nature vs. Nurture

One of the biggest fallacies in capitalistic theory is the idea that we are who we are only because of what we decide to do with our lives. While we would like to believe our lives and personal situation is the result of our own doing, one has to consider factors of chance and the effect our environment has had on us. It is what we do with those chances that help to shape our prospects in life. Therefore, our present situation in life is based on a mixture of both nature and nurture.

Even if we do well because of our own hard work and genius, there is another false assumption that conservatives like to believe and use as an excuse to support pure capitalistic ideals. They say, "I've earned it, why should I pay more taxes?" This statement could be wholly true if we believe our situation is the exclusive result of our own doing; if we assume that it is our own genius and hard work that puts us where we are. But guess what? No one who is wealthy has done it 100% on their own. Do you think that someone born in Rwanda would have had the same chance to achieve the same riches as someone in the U.S. based solely on their hard work? While many who have succeeded needed to be smart and work hard, they have also had help from their environment whether they recognize it or not. Warren Buffet understands and recognizes the impact environment has had on his success, stating that if he was born in Bangladesh there is no way he would have been able to accomplish what he has.[viii]

America and the American dream has been made possible because of the environment we created together that allows businesses to thrive and people to do well. The wealthy have become so not just because of hard work, but also because of the environment they were able to do it in. Public education that creates an educated pool of workers, all other necessary infrastructure paid for with tax dollars and access to the open market, has all helped people obtain wealth for themselves. For anyone to say they completely made it on their own is delusional and can't see how tax dollars have helped create the environment they live in, allowing them to do so well. Could Steve Jobs or Bill Gates have amassed immense wealth if they had no one to sell their products too? What if they didn't have the educated programmers to help develop their innovations? Let's not forget the roads that are used to help deliver their products. If it was not for our patent protection laws, ideas could easily be stolen, devaluing the worth of their innovations and products. They say it takes a community to raise a child. Well, it also takes a community to raise a business.

Majority Rule While Protecting the Minority

Proposition 8 was a voter referendum that was passed by a majority of citizen's votes in California, denying homosexual couples the right to marry. The courts however just overturned this law on the grounds that the law was unconstitutional. Some were very pleased to hear this news, but not surprisingly many others especially the commentators at FOX news were upset.

Not only was the ruling a big step forward for the issues concerning gay rights, it showed that there is a lot more to our democracy than just the ideas of freedom and voting. What sets us apart from most other countries that call themselves a democracy is not just the idea that a majority vote wins, but even more importantly is that we protect the rights of the minority. Government in the United States is ruled by the majority, but still protects the rights of the minority.

This doesn't only mean minorities as other races, religions or such, but also includes any group of people whose ideals may be different from the majority. If Republicans are in power then Democrats are the current minority and vice versa. Our system is set up such that if one party or group is in power they cannot simply impose their ideals on everyone else regardless.

Back to the example of Proposition 8: A majority of Californians voted to ban same sex marriage. After passing the referendum, this new law was challenged in our judicial system and overturned by a conservative panel of judges, upsetting lots of people. Many seemed unable to understand how a few judges could overturn something that was voted on by seven million people. Again the thing that makes our country great is that it doesn't matter if a majority is in favor of something. If it opposes or infringes on the rights of the minority then it is unconstitutional. Period!

To give another example let's look at a similar situation that fell in favor of the conservative viewpoint on gun control. In the Democratic controlled state of Illinois and in the city of Chicago, which has a heavily Democratic population, a ban on handguns was imposed 30 years ago. This ban certainly angered many Republicans and the NRA. In 2010 the Supreme Court declared the ban unconstitutional. It is in the Bill of Rights that we all have the right to bear arms. Just because you may live in an area where a majority of people want to outlaw guns does not mean they can simply vote to ban guns. This is the beauty of our system of balance working.

The only way the right to own a gun can ever be revoked is by an amendment to the Constitution. This would require not a 51% majority but a super majority of votes; meaning 75% of Congress would have to be in favor of any change to the Constitution.   Since the judges declared California's ban on gay marriage unconstitutional, means that a super majority in Congress would also be needed to place an outright ban gay marriage. This is the system of checks and balances working in our country, protecting the rights of the minority despite the will of the majority.

Chapter 4

Balancing our Debates

Equal Vs. Equal Opportunity

There is one thing to be said about being equal: We are all humans! No matter our differences, we are all human beings with equal needs and should all have equal rights. Under our Constitution, based on the fact that we are all equal human beings with equal needs, the government has a responsibility to ensure that the rights of every citizen is protected equally.

Does this mean we should all be granted an equal income or an equal standard of living? Of course not! It would be nice if we each had the best possible standard of living and that is what we strive for. Under capitalism we are all free to work and strive to be the best we can. Our capitalistic system entices us to work hard, so we may achieve that high standard of living. (Further discussion on Standard of Living in Chapter 7) Should a high standard of living be automatically granted to everyone? Not at all. We get what we work for! Should those who are lazy be afforded the same standard of living as those who do work hard and put forth more effort? Of course not! These are some of the core beliefs behind capitalism that most people would agree with. It is what we are all taught as Americans. Work hard and you will do well.

But why is this not always the case? Why can two equal people do the same thing, put forth the same amount of effort and not receive the same returns? It is because there is a lack of equal opportunity.

Is it enough for our government to simply state and recognize that we are all equal? According to the theory of capitalism, the free markets and their outcomes will balance themselves when there is something called "perfect competition." Perfect competition is the need for private companies to have equal business opportunities in order for the market to stay balanced. If one company has an unfair advantage such as preferred access to a raw material, then that company's advantage will upset the balance of competition. Chances are that a business with an unfair advantage will overtake and do better in the market. This means a company with preferred treatment will probably put others out of business, becoming the leader in that industry, eventually turning into a monopoly, which disrupts the balance of competition in that market.

So too this idea of perfect competition can be compared to the competition among individuals, in that we all should have equal opportunities to prosper. Not to say all people will prosper due to the fact that some will work harder than others, some will be better or smarter at certain things than others. But a balance of wealth can be achieved where people earn a living proportionate to the amount of work, goods, or innovations that they put into the system.

However this achieved balance, based on the idea of perfect competition can only be reached if there is an equal opportunity for those in the market place to compete. The same capitalistic theory of perfect competition for businesses could also be applied to individuals, which translates to equal opportunity for all.

In order to have a balance of wealth where you are rewarded proportionately to the work you put in, everyone needs to have that initial equal opportunity. Many in this country will say we are all free to do well which is enough to guarantee equal opportunity. We are all free to rise above. But this is clearly not the reality.

In business, if there is a company that already owns a big market share, it is tough and often impossible for a new business to emerge in that industry and do well. It may be possible, but only in extraordinary cases. Most of the time if a new business prospers it is because of a shift in the market; a new technology emerges, demand grows, or a company gains some other advantage or new innovation that wasn't there before. So too is the case for individuals. Can anyone agree that Paris Hilton has had the same opportunities as a child born into poverty? Do they both have the same opportunity to go to a good school? Does the person who has to work at an early age in order to pay for the basics of living, take away from their ability to learn and do better? Clearly Paris Hilton and an impoverished child haven't had equal opportunities. While there are some who were born into poverty and able to rise up to great wealth and riches, only a few outliers were able to do so.

To take the example even further, look at the saying "it takes money to make money." Of course someone who already has wealth and resources has a great advantage over someone who doesn't.

Do children born into poverty have the same opportunity to attend a good school as someone like Paris Hilton? Of course not! A basic minimum education is needed so that everyone has the opportunity to do well. Public education also helps create an environment for "perfect competition" among individuals, so that we may have a "balanced market" of people.

Under the beliefs of extreme capitalists, education should be privatized for profit as everything else. In our current system of socialized public schools, an impoverished child is able to go to school, which helps give them an equal opportunity. But for those who support extreme capitalism and privatized schools, the child born into poverty may not be able to afford a basic education and hence wouldn't have an equal opportunity to do well in life. If everyone in society has the ability to gain an education, isn't this a way to help provide equal opportunity? Couldn't this be considered part of the government's mandate to ensure the general welfare of our country?

More and more extremists on the right support the idea of privatized schools. But if people can't afford it, denying children a basic education that supports equal opportunity, how can we achieve the "perfect competition" needed in a capitalistic society to obtain balanced markets? It is this idea of perfect competition among individuals that allow people to receive rewards proportionate to the work they put in.

No one is guaranteed wealth, but we can only create it for ourselves if we have the opportunity to do so. Public education is just one part of helping to create that equal opportunity.

Debating the Debate

Part of the problem plaguing our government today is the inability to come up with workable solutions, falling short on good ideas because we stick to extremist ideals or philosophies. One of the big issues we face today is that of deficit reduction. Extreme Republicans believe spending cuts that promote their ideals of capitalism is the only way forward. Extreme Liberals believe that raising revenue in the form of taxes is the only solution.

People with extreme views have worked their way into the political system pushing our leaders into a culture of partisan politics. They frame their ideas and beliefs as good and the other's belief system as bad, leaving no room for compromise.

Even though most Americans would be considered moderate, people using extreme political viewpoints have framed the issues for the American people to understand as good or bad. They say, "Capitalism is good, socialism is bad. Taxes are bad, free markets are good. Government spending is bad."

When debating an issue by using these absolute frames, distracts us from having any constructive debate about particular issues that need to be addressed. For example, anything that has to do with "spending" is labeled by an extreme capitalist as a sign of bigger government, which has been framed as bad. When using general arguments such as "government spending is bad," the debate is diverted from the issue at hand.

Consider spending on a project to fix and expand an old highway, which would put people to work and enable businesses to operate more effectively. When somebody simply argues against the project because it involves spending money, automatically the debate is no longer about the issue; "Do we need to expand this highway?" Now the debate has been shifted to the issue concerning "the size of government", which is not what is being debated in this example. When discussing the need for this highway, the moment someone says "No" to the project because "we want to decrease spending," automatically the debate is no longer about the potential <u>need</u> for the project, but has been diverted again to the issue concerning the size of government.

A specific example was the debate or lack there of, concerning the recent healthcare law passed by Congress. I could hardly find anyone in the major news media commentating in depth on the actual pros or cons of actual provisions that were in the law. Instead we heard most arguing the law in severely generalized terms and frames. It was called a "socialist policy," with bigger government spending and government intrusion into our personal lives. Little was mentioned concerning the actual details of the bill. Few people looked into the particulars asking questions such as; would the law actually help lower overall healthcare costs; or if the law would help people gain access to healthcare. Instead politicians and pundits fed us general frames with their own connotations.

These tactics used by politicians during deliberations have hampered our efforts to come up with any reasonable, workable solutions. Another issue where these general framing tactics are used can be seen in the debate regarding our immigration problems. Using key terms or frames that are simply labeled as good or bad disrupt the possibility of coming up with any good ideas. The extreme left has deemed that any law or regulation put forth against illegal immigrants would be "racist" and "discriminatory" towards Mexicans and Latinos. The extreme right has concluded that anything other than full prosecution would be a form of "amnesty" which undermines our laws and law-abiding citizens. We are stuck in a stalemate where nothing is done and no workable solutions arise due to extreme thinking. Continued use of simple frames distracts from forming any constructive debate.

One group says "No to amnesty!" which sounds good and another group says "Stop discrimination!" which also sounds good. Both of these phrases have merit that most everyone could agree with. But the problem being debated isn't "discrimination" or "amnesty". The problem is illegal immigration! We need a new way to address the issues when we debate. Workable solutions can only be reached by first recognizing the beliefs and values of most Americans pertaining to this problem.

Forget about politics for a moment or anything other than the issue of immigration and see if you agree with the statements below.

1. *We don't want any policy to be unfairly discriminatory to one race.*
2. *We don't want to simply grant rights to illegal immigrants, which undermine those who are law-abiding immigrants.*
3. *We don't want American workers to continue to compete with cheap labor: a labor force paid under the minimum wage and not taxed (referred to as "under the table").*
4. *We don't want to suddenly eliminate a workforce that many businesses have been utilizing, creating a sudden shock to the economy.*
5. *We don't want the continuation of a situation that supports illegal activity, which continues to be a humanitarian disaster due to people dying while trying to cross the border and people living in substandard conditions while hiding.*

I'm sure most Americans can agree with all the statements listed above. If Republicans and Democrats can agree on these statements, then we are that much closer to finding a solution.

Now that we have made statements most people can agree on, we can look to come up with a true solution without simply arguing "No to amnesty" or "Stop Discrimination". Here is the start of one possible resolution. It may not perfect, but it could be workable by taking into consideration all of the statements listed above.

First, all illegal immigrants must register their jobs if they have one within a given time period. Then they must leave the country within that time period and apply for a proper visa, where they will be automatically allowed to return to the U.S. using that registered job on their visa application. After the allowed time period to register your job and leave the country, if you are still in the U.S. illegally you will be prosecuted and deported. This proposition doesn't automatically grant amnesty, nor is it an unyielding heavy hand. And of course after initiating this program there needs to be more done to secure the borders.

This is just an example of a possible solution. One

that is modeled after a successful policy Malaysia initiated back in the 1990s in response to their issue concerning a large influx of illegal Indonesians. Thousands of Indonesians were entering Malaysia illegally, taking up jobs as maids and laborers; similar to the problem we have today with illegal aliens from Mexico. I believe an idea like this helps solve the problem while taking into account all of the concerns we listed above. It doesn't simply discriminate or grant amnesty. A program like this won't allow for cheap labor as employers will be subject to labor laws and it will generate more tax revenue for a border protection program. A solution like this doesn't wipe out a labor force and it doesn't undermine law-abiding immigrants.

Again, not to say this is a perfect idea or solution, but at least it is one that tries to take into account all of our common beliefs. However, such a solution will never be reached if we allow extremists to continue to debate issues using only frames such as "No to Amnesty!" Broad terms that we label as good or bad used in a debate distract from the issues at hand. Amnesty in this situation is considered "bad". Therefore anything that falls short of rounding up illegal immigrants for deportation is seen as a form of amnesty, and hence opposed by the right.

How the religious became Right?

Recently I have found myself asking this question: How can religion and more specifically, Christians who talk of morals and good Christian charity, wholly support the conservative right? How can they support a conservative party whose main guiding philosophy of capitalism leaves those who are less fortunate in poverty to fend for themselves, without any help from society? How can good Christians support a party that looks to eliminate entitlements for those who actually do need the assistance due to circumstances beyond their control? I understand the need to try and stop freeloaders from gaming the system, which is a different issue. But to get rid of all these programs that do help those in need, seems morally incomprehensible.

One of the principles which allows capitalism to

flourish is our belief in the need to reward hard work. If you work hard you will do well. So we assume it to be true, that hard work pays off. We also assume the opposite to be true, that if you are lazy you will not receive as good a fortune.

This is one of the driving principles behind capitalism. Hard work= doing well. Laziness= being poor. While this is what we believe and hope to be true, it is not always the case. Being taught these rules from young has distorted our views of what actually happens to many people around us. People tend to automatically assume that if you are rich, then you must have worked hard and if you are poor then it means you are lazy. Yes, many who are wealthy are so because of hard work and many who are poor are so because of laziness. However not everyone fits neatly into these categories. There are some who are wealthy due to means other than their hard work and there are those poor who have worked hard, but due to circumstances beyond their control remain poor. No matter how hard they try they can't seem to get out of poverty.

Most of what I am talking about here goes back to our earlier discussion concerning the importance of equal opportunity. In order for people's class and income to be based on the amount of work they put in, there has to be an equal opportunity for everyone.

But there is another factor that helps determine our status and situation, which many of us don't consider: Chance! We like to believe that we are the masters of our own lives; that we get what we deserve. Again, many of us grew up with the idea that hard work pays off. But what about people who are rich that didn't work for it? More importantly, what about people who are poor due to no fault of their own? Who are these people? I'm talking about the millions of kids who grow up in the ghetto from a broken family, who were kept out of school most of their childhood and never given the tools to get ahead. What about the average worker, who one day is doing well, then suddenly falls terminally ill? In this situation someone can easily get bogged down with medical bills, no longer being able to work, while their kids and family fall into poverty. What does capitalism and the Christian conservatives who support the right say for someone in this situation? According to pure capitalism there is no compassion or help for those who would be in poverty for no fault of their own. I'm not one who is interested in helping those who are lazy that don't want to help themselves. But just because you may have a group of people who are poor, doesn't mean they are all poor for the same reason.

When we talk of entitlements most conservatives see them as free rides for the lazy. Most liberals and I see entitlements as compassionate assistance for those who cannot help themselves. In this debate it is important to separate those who need help and those who take assistance without the desire to improve their situation. We have both types of people, but the point here again is to find a balance. In order to make balanced, fair and compassionate policy, we need to recognize both points of view. First, that we don't want to reward laziness and second, that there are those people who need help that can't help themselves. When we recognize both views we can begin to effectively craft programs with rules that don't allow the lazy to take advantage of a situation and at the same time provides compassionate assistance to those who really deserve and need it. I can't understand how it is that those who would claim to be moral Christians will support a political party whose conservative philosophy looks to deny help to those who need it most.

Last year Paul Ryan, the Republican leader of the House Budget Committee issued his ideas for a federal budget. His budget plan drastically slashed funds for programs such as Food Stamps, Housing and Urban Development, Welfare, and Unemployment insurance to name a few.[ix] I was very pleased when a few months ago, the Catholic bishops came out against the Ryan Budget plan; a plan that looked to severely reduce most government programs designed to help the unfortunate. Maybe there is hope for religion to denounce the views of the extreme right who have claimed to be the party of moral, religious principles.

When it comes to entitlements and programs for the less fortunate, we can shape policy to make sure money isn't wasted on freeloaders, while still preserving the original intentions of these programs designed to assist those who really need help the most. We should not simply use examples of freeloaders as an excuse to cut funding, denying help to those who really do need it.

Shifting the Center: Why do they call it the Liberal Media?

In our country we always had and always will have our political divisions. Not everyone is the same with the same viewpoints. It's a good thing too. It makes for a dynamic society when you have opposing views. Constructive discussions can hopefully occur between opposing parties in order to strike a balance of ideas that can benefit everyone. In the political spectrum we have The Right, The Left and all those who fall in-between.

From the 1950s through the end of the 1980s we had the Cold war with Russia.   During this time Americans bound together in a common cause and were able to accomplish some great tasks. Funding for NASA as part of the Space Race and the development of our military were direct results of the Cold war. Our support for these initiatives led to other offshoot industries, which NASA and military technologies helped to create. (More on this in Chapter 9) After the end of the Cold War, when there was no longer a binding cause that all Americans could rally behind, our ideals and the political arena started to change. Unfortunately our change wasn't for the better.

A new extreme breed of Republican started emerging in the philosophies of Donald Rumsfeld, Ronald Reagan, Paul Wolfowitz, Dick Cheney and Karl Rove just to name a few. Their goal was to move the country further to the right. They saw that over the course of the 20th century, since the Great Depression, that America had moved its ideals towards the left. These Republicans wanted to move the country back the other direction. (I would argue that those wealthy few with the funds to help this movement along have largely contributed to this shift towards the right, which is another topic we will examine later.)

What was the process used to try and achieve shifting the center or a majority of people's thoughts towards the right? The conservatives decided to start picking up far right ideals, shouting them as loud and as sternly as they could.

Don't believe that the Republicans moved further to the right? Let's look at some examples of older Republican Presidents. In 1956 President Eisenhower undertook a major spending initiative by starting the Interstate Highway Project. In 1970 Richard Nixon formed the Environmental Protection Agency. President Ford, in a time of economic recession imposed a one-year, 5% tax increase on corporations and the wealthy. Could you imagine any of today's Republicans proposing or even supporting any of these measures? All these initiatives led by Republican presidents, seem, like proposals that would only be initiated by today's Democrats.

The Republicans of today, by moving their agenda further to the right away from the center, creates more space between them and the center. By moving further to the right, all ideas that were moderate seem further to the left. Today, the supposed independent media that was reporting from the center seems further to the left as well.

To counteract this move to the right, liberals on the left figured the only way to react to this shift, was for them to move more extreme to the left.

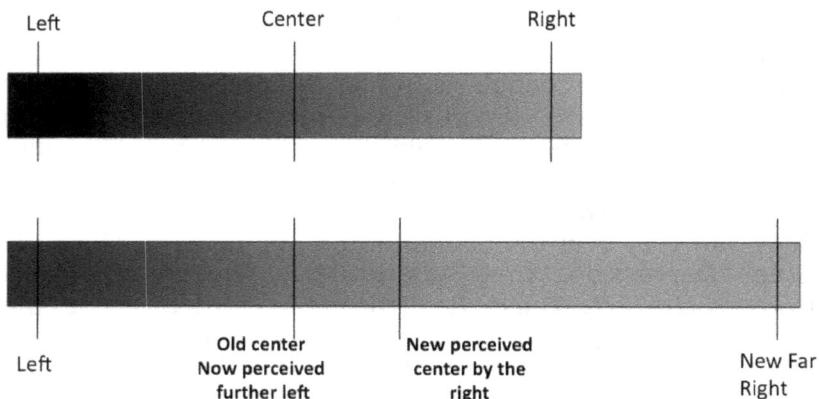

We have the obvious polarized media outlets of FOX, headed by the ultra-conservative Rupert Murdoch, and MSNBC certainly pushing back from the far left. But what about the rest of the media who try to preserve journalistic integrity, independent of politics, unbiased, reporting from the center? If today's media were to report in an unbiased manner, giving attention to Republican President, Richard Nixon and his proposals for forming the EPA in 1970, today's Republicans would scream liberal bias.

Naming Our Fears. The Results of Extremism

Many see their viewpoint as correct and the opposite's viewpoint as wrong. We become fearful of what can occur if the opposing ideology takes form in its extreme.

Conservatives fear and foresee the following issues if extreme liberal laws are passed. These fears are not without merit as we have seen occur before in history, with the extreme socialistic policies of the former Soviet Union and other communist countries.

Conservative fears of Extreme Socialism:
-No ownership of private property
-Lack of profit motive
-Hard workers supporting the lazy
-Lack of individual freedom
-Little to no economic growth

Just as conservatives have their fears of an extreme socialist agenda, so too liberals have their own fears of a nation based on extreme conservative and purely capitalistic ideologies. The fears of liberals also have their merit based in history. We have seen the problems that extreme, unregulated capitalism has led to in the past such as the U.S. Great Depression and mass poverty in South America during the 1970s.

Liberal fears of Extreme Capitalism:
-Increases in wealth disparity
-Stifles equal opportunity
-No protections for health and safety
-Pure profit motives that go against the collective good

49

Assuming we all agree on the common goals mentioned in the first chapter then we should also agree that no one wishes any of the above listed "fears" to transpire. This is why we must fight extremism at all cost and must recognize the fears of others. We need to see how our own ideologies practiced in their extreme forms can hinder reaching our common goals.

Whichever direction on the political spectrum you personally lean towards, there are extreme forms of your beliefs. If you are a Democrat or Republican, even though you may be moderate and agree with all the common principles we laid out in the first chapter, you must realize that there is an even extremer form of your ideology on your side of the political spectrum. We must recognize the fears of the other side, those who fear your ideologies in their extreme forms. In order to make an argument towards someone with an opposing view, you must first recognize their fears that could arise from your ideology practiced in its extreme form and reaffirm them of our common American goals.

Let's take an example such as the issue of welfare funding. Moderate conservatives may feel that it is wasteful to spend on those who are lazy freeloaders and so will support defunding such a program. Moderate liberals can see the benefits to fund these programs in order to help those in need. Defunding welfare will seem to Democrats as a step towards the extreme right view of ending welfare all together. Republicans will see a liberal plan to increase funding as a waste. They fear an extreme move towards a situation where the government steals from the rich to give to the poor and lazy, enabling more people to become lazy.

The truth is neither extreme ideal should be sought. By recognizing our common goals and the fears of our opponents we can work towards a true compromise. With increased funding for welfare, in order to quell the fears of conservatives, stricter standards can be imposed to help ensure that the money goes to those who really need it. Further programs can be implemented in conjunction with welfare to help people rise out of poverty and not continue to depend on welfare.

The right, if wanting to cut spending, should do so by showing areas of wasteful spending and offer ways to make the program more efficient. Agreements can be made where everyone is assured that neither extreme will come to pass; where welfare is neither eradicated completely, nor will it be allowed to grow into a massive government handout that people take advantage of, allowing the lazy to live off of the fruit of other's labor. But to reach such a compromise we must first recognize and address the fears of people with opposing viewpoints.

Chapter 5

Economies Unbalanced

Monopoly, it's not just a game!

Monopolies. For those of you that aren't sure what a Monopoly is, here's the definition:

Monopoly: to have exclusive control or ownership by one party over a commodity.

There are many reasons based on both capitalism and socialism that we view monopolies as something that is not good for society. Monopolies hamper competition and should be regulated in order to promote freedom in the market and support the well being of society.

Under "laissez-faire" policies (government hands off) or extreme capitalism, monopolies are allowed to form and run free. One company controlling an entire industry for its own benefit, without government regulation results in sky rocketing prices and a stifling of competition. There are many instances throughout history where this practice has occurred and ended in anti-trust lawsuits. Two of our country's biggest and most famous monopolies were that of Standard Oil, which was broken up in 1909 and AT&T, which was split apart in 1987. Also, just last year AT&T tried merging with T-Mobile. The acquisition was stopped by the Justice Department due to fears of a lack of competition in the communications market.

In an unregulated free market place, the eventual formation of monopolies within every industry would occur. For those who don't agree just look at the game of Monopoly. You play and play the game till someone wins. How do you win? You win by eventually owning all the properties and having all the money, while everyone else is left with nothing.

If the simple game of Monopoly isn't convincing enough, look around at the real industries of the world. Let's start with the airlines. Northwest Airlines bought Midwest Airlines. Then Delta Airlines recently bought Northwest. Continental Airlines bought Frontier and then merged with United Airlines, which already bought over many regional carriers. US Airways merged with America West and recently looked to merge with American Airlines. Over the years this could continue until there is one company left standing. This probably would have happened already if the government had not interfered in certain cases. United's bid to take over US Air back in 2000 is just one case that was stopped by the Justice Department.

However, our government seems to have allowed the formation of bigger companies at an exponential rate over the past 40 years. We are in the age of mega conglomerates, where there are only a few companies left at the top of every major industry. Television, broadcast, bank, airline, automobile, and newspaper industries all have only a few top controlling companies. The only reason there are still about four or five different mega companies within each industry and not just one monopoly is because of government interference in the form of anti-trust laws.

If anyone out there doesn't see a problem with the formation of mega conglomerates, look no further than the banking industry, where we have allowed a few "mega banks" to form, which became "too big to fail." Even allowing industries to only have four or five top dogs still stifles competition and allows for private industry to fix prices as oligopolies or cartels. (Where only a few parties control a commodity.)

The top five oil companies is a perfect example of a cartel. Speculation, similar survival interests and a lack of competition allows for these five top companies to operate as if it was one when it comes to consumer prices and lobbying the government for preferential treatment.

Then there are the dangers to our very democracy by allowing our news and information, which is controlled by private companies, to be in the hands of one company. 95% of our major mass media is already controlled by a small handful of large corporations. This includes radio stations, TV broadcast, newspaper, film, and print medias. The infusion of technology, mostly being cable and now the Internet, has added new markets and new competition. But the buying frenzy from the top media conglomerates has allowed the formation of even bigger mega-conglomerates. New cable TV stations continue to get bought up by the big three TV providers. We also have the Internet war, which is still fairly new but expanding with large companies like Google and Microsoft becoming media conglomerates of their own.

If a lack of government regulation supported by extreme capitalism allows monopolies to form, but the existence of monopolies hampers competition and fair pricing that is needed for capitalism to function, how do we deal with this paradox?

Simply put, there must be some form of government regulation to ensure the balance of a free market place. Regulations that reward hard work, allow for growth, encourages competition, and prevents unfair practices are all needed to ensure fair and balanced markets. But isn't government interference and regulations a form of socialism? Yes, it is.

We have had a balance of capitalism and socialism at work for generations where we are able to maintain our principles of freedom, while protecting the good of society at the same time.

How do we regulate without hampering the freedoms of individuals or businesses? A full meaningful discussion can and must occur in order to figure out just the right balance of regulation and free market practices. However, we should be mindful of extremists who would frame the arguments using all or nothing terms. There can be no constructive discussion when politicians talk, using only general terms like "government should get out of the way of business," without recognizing our fears of a world with no government regulations. And that fear is living in a world of monopolies.

The one ticket theory

In a free society with a capitalistic marketplace, we are taught that prices for goods and services are based on supply and demand. Since coming up in the music business and being an entrepreneur in college myself, I needed to use these capitalistic principles all the time.

There is a general rule called the 80/20 split that is

used in many aspects of business. In the concert business an 80/20 split was used as a typical assumption for budgeting; that all pricing, budgeting costs, and revenues would be based on selling 80% of tickets in any given venue. Deals were made between artists and promoters that assumed selling 80% of a venue's capacity would cover everyone's costs and the extra 20% was profit to be split among the artists and promoters. They would still negotiate ahead of time who would assume what part of the risks, costs, and rewards, but the main point is that budgeting was based on being able to sell 80% of the house.

Assuming that costs, ticket prices and budgeting were set based on this standard 80/20 theory, you could look at a typical concert crowd and figure if the promoter was making money or not. If the house were less than 80% full, we'd figure someone was losing money. If the show was more than 80% full we could be sure the promoter was making money. This was standard concert business practice for years and then a new system with new practices emerged; one based on support from large corporate profits and a new wealthy class of people.

Clear Channel Entertainment became one of the world's largest concert promoters after years of buyouts and takeovers. After becoming a near monopoly they started a new business practice that had nothing to do with the standard 80/20 split that guided the concert business for so long. Now due to the company's large size and huge reserves of cash, they were able to offer artists large guarantees. They would offer artists large sums of money at a loss to themselves, simply so they could put other promoters out of business. Once most of the competition was out of business, Clear Channel was free to set ticket prices to their liking in order to make more money, free of competition.

All of a sudden ticket prices for events started soaring. Tickets to see bands such as the Eagles when they first rejoined cost $500. Tickets for average bands that teenagers would buy, which used to cost $30-$40 now cost $100-$200. Why? Because now the promoters found a way of making the most money possible without competition! Before, promoters would care about filling the house in order to please the artists, cover their costs and make a profit, while still being aware of the need to be competitive. How could I sell the most tickets? I would set my price as high as I thought I could and still fill every seat.

Now the promoters don't care about filling every seat. A typical concert, in a standard hockey arena for a well-known national artist could earn about 1.2 million dollars selling out with 16,000 tickets. Promoters figured out over the past few years that they could charge more, sell fewer tickets and still make more money. Instead of selling 16,000 tickets at an average of $75 dollars they could find enough people to buy $200 tickets and would only need to sell 8,000 tickets to make more money. Now kids and many fans that can't afford the $200 tickets don't get a chance to go to the shows. We could go on to say that Clear Channel could sell one ticket for 1.2 million dollars, make their money and be happy. And in fact this does happen.

All the time in the music business, artists more and more are looking towards making money from the one corporate show that pays exuberant amounts of money for a private party by a wealthy CEO and his ten closest friends. No longer is the market in the music industry about reaching as many fans as possible, but about trying to make money off the wealthy few.

This situation concerning concert ticket prices is just one example of what can occur under monopolistic practices. This is also why Clear Channel spun off its concert division amid complaints and fears of anti-trust actions.[x] In this example where Clear Channel has charged more in order to provide less, also occurs throughout other industries as well. Imagine the same situation occurring in markets that provide things we need such as food, clothing and shelter. This brings us to our next topic, which explores the other reasons why we need a balance of government controls over businesses and markets.

Faults in the law of Supply and Demand
When Laissez-Faire doesn't work!

The law of supply and demand is fairly simple to understand. It states that when demand is high and or supply is down then prices go up. And the reverse holds true; as demand goes down for a product or service, or if supplies are in surplus than prices fall. These are basic rules that function at the core of capitalism. Extreme capitalists believe that everything, all goods and services should be privately owned, adhering to the laws of supply and demand. But there are a few instances where the law of supply and demand doesn't hold to be true. If left to its own devices, capitalism driven by the laws of supply and demand can collapse an economy, ignoring the common good of society and our country. The law of supply and demand fails to provide for the good of the country when:

1. *When there is a large gap between rich and poor.*
2. *When there is a product or service that all humans demand out of necessity (e.g. food, shelter, healthcare)*
3. *When there is a demand for large infrastructure, which neither individuals nor individual businesses can afford themselves.*
4. *When there are public needs but no market to profit from.*

Let's first look at what happens in an economy where there is a huge gap between rich and poor. What happens to health care for example when there is a large disparity of wealth? When there is a wider gap between rich and poor, prices can inflate higher and higher. Certain goods and services that were once affordable by a middle class, no longer are. Let's look at an example with a simple business plan working to maximize profit.

Assume a company is selling cars at $10,000 a piece and sells 100 cars to produce one million dollars in revenue. But what if that company could start charging $25,000 per car? They would only have to sell 40 cars to earn the same revenue and can reduce their costs at the same time by producing less. Due to a high wealth disparity, they were able to find 40 people from the higher income bracket that were willing and able to pay $25,000. Here the company only had to make 40 cars instead of 100 to earn the same amount of revenue. Therefore, they were able to cut production costs and still earn the same amount. Other car companies catch onto this idea and now the average car costs $15,000 more. So, out of the original hundred people who would have liked to buy a car at $10,000, instead only 40 people were able to buy the cars and 60 people can no longer afford them. The car manufacturers were able to minimize costs, charge more and earn a higher profit by fixing their prices towards the higher income brackets, leaving the middle class no longer able to afford these products.

Now apply the same example to other goods or services that are provided by companies who operate with a profit motive: Healthcare, telephone, utilities, housing, merchandise, supplies. What happens when this occurs in industries that supply essential needs? As companies are able to raise prices due to the inequity of income, (earning more by producing less), more and more people are not able to afford these products and are pushed further into poverty. This cycle reinforces itself, driving the gap between rich and poor wider and wider. As prices inflate less and less people can afford to buy.

This practice of maximizing profits by charging more and producing less can be seen in almost every industry. Over the past ten years the average price of a car has doubled. Healthcare costs have risen. Industries relating to travel such as airline tickets and hotel rooms around the world have raised their prices, maximizing profits based off of corporate customers, deciding to no longer cater to the middle class. The price of entertainment such as concerts has doubled, the reasons for which I have shown in the previous section about the "1 Ticket Theory". Now due to the growing gap between rich and poor only a select portion of music fans can afford the $60 minimum price to see their favorite artist. (In the concert industry I came from, it didn't take an economics professor to see something was awry as Alicia Key's popularity grew and hence her ticket prices. Her audiences, which use to be predominantly kids from more urbanized backgrounds, slowly changed to an audience that was predominately upper middle class, white.)

Does this mean that companies and businesses shouldn't be free to maximize profits? Not at all. What it does mean is that when a government supports policies that allow for a growing divide between rich and poor, you will get high inflation, resulting in growing poverty that increases exponentially and in the end a failing economy.

This is what has happened in the recent housing crash. Market prices were driven up to a level that most people could no longer afford. This is especially true in towns and regions where the wealthy have flooded the market, driving up prices. Many will say I am wrong; that the housing crash was due to banks selling "bad securities" or "bad debt". This is true, but what is a "bad security" or "bad debt"? Simply put, it is a mortgage that an individual can't afford. As millions of American's incomes remained stagnant and the cost of living gradually increased, they could no longer afford the rising cost of homes. Plain and simple. Then of course there are the millions who overnight lost their jobs, reinforcing the affordability problem.

Another instance where the law of supply and demand fails and threatens the well being of society is when there is a product or service that is demanded by all. Let's use the example of utilities such as electricity and water. Under our current system there are some publicly owned utilities that operate as not-for-profit, government-owned organizations. There are also privately owned utilities, but because most are a monopoly in their region and there is a demand from everyone in society, the government regulates them and their prices. Should these companies be allowed to operate without price regulations? Under an uncontrolled monopoly, in a laissez-faire world, prices would skyrocket. This is why we have always had government regulations over public utilities that everybody needs. I find it hard to believe that most Americans would be in favor of deregulating monopolistic companies, especially utilities where prices would increase for all. I have yet to see a business model where a monopoly, if left to their own devices would lower prices.

Then there are instances where there is a need by

society but no market to profit from. Examples of such needs would be the benefits of forest preservation. Protecting the land, our waterways, ecosystems, and conserving natural resources are all examples of society's needs that offer little profit motive. Our institutions that provide security such as our prison system, has little profit to be made in a purely capitalistic society without public funding. How does the law of supply and demand affect these things we need, when there is no profit to be made from it.   Without government regulation and socialistic programs such as the National Forestry, private companies would be free to benefit from these resources, driven only by profit motive and not the public good. I am not saying that private companies should not be able to run a forestry project, but the law of supply and demand would say that there is a demand for these trees and so we should harvest them for a profit. Left to their own devices, a private company has no motive to conserve a forest or preserve ecosystems. Social regulation is required in order to balance the capitalistic motives of such a company that is in contrast with what is good for the country as a whole.

What about our prison system? Our current prison system does have issues and there are many factors involved that could be better handled. There have been a few instances where private companies have run prisons for a profit and they have failed! In 2008, there were two juvenile correction facilities owned and operated by a private company in Wilkes-Barre, Pennsylvania. It was found that the owners were bribing local judges to issue harsher and longer sentences to kids who came through their courtroom.[xi] This is what occurs in the "for-profit" prison system. Of course the best thing for a private company that owns a prison would be high crime. The more criminals, the more money they make. Their interests are to have increased crime, longer and stricter sentences for criminals and would place less emphasis on rehabilitation, all things that work against the common good of society. And who pays the private, for-profit prisons? The taxpayer still does. The government gives the private company an allotment for each prisoner, same as our school system. In order to make more money, a privately owned prison company would want more people to commit crime.

As a country we already have many socialist laws and policies to protect against instances where the law of supply and demand works against the welfare of society. The important point to stress here is the balance between views. Capitalism should be allowed to work, helping people build better lives but at the same time ensuring the public good of society as a whole. We need to protect the freedoms of businesses and individuals, while at the same time using policy to ensure the common good. This cannot be achieved by a purely "laissez-faire" approach to government.

Part III
Yesterday, Today and Tomorrow

Chapter 6

Taxes and Their Effects

A bit of scary economic facts-

Here is where I would like to switch gears and talk more specifically about our economy and taxes. Tax policy can have a dramatic effect on our economy as a whole. In this section we will look at specific tax policies, tax rates and how they affect our economy. After researching some facts and figures I was able to find some startling trends.

Before we can look at how taxes affect the economy, we need to come up with a control group. We need an ideal! What is our country's economic goal? What does the ideal economic situation in a free-market economy look like? What would that ideal situation look like on a graph? After we've established what the ideal economic situation should look like, then we can examine where we have been economically as a country and if we are moving away or towards that economic goal which we established as the ideal.

Once our ideal has been established and we have seen the direction our economy has moved in respect to that ideal, finally we can look at factors such as taxes that have helped to push our economy towards or away from that ideal situation.

For my study I focused on trends that have occurred since 1960. To show you these trends, all numbers are researched in five-year increments. If someone has the time to do the same study in more detail, looking at numbers for every year, I would gladly welcome the assistance.

The main numbers we will examine here are Gross Domestic Product or GDP and Median Household Income which I will use the acronym MHI. Gross Domestic Product or GDP is the total amount in dollars that our country produces and hence earns. We often look towards GDP as an indicator of the health of our nation. As GDP goes up, we say the economy is growing which is a sign of a healthy, growing economy.

However GDP alone does not give us the full picture of

our economic situation as a whole country. One person out of millions can earn all the money in our country, increasing his earnings alone raising our overall GDP, while everyone else remains poor. As an example, if the U.S. GDP grew this year by 10% does that mean it's a good thing? Especially if only one person in the country saw all the benefits from that 10% growth? We would hope that as GDP grows most people's income would grow as well.

So, we can't just look at GDP as a gage for the health of our economy. This is where Median Household Income comes in to play. MHI is the amount that the family in the middle of the spectrum makes. If you marked everyone's income in a line from bottom to top, the Median Household Income would be represented by the income of the person in the middle of that line. Half of the people in society would earn more and half of the people would earn less.

In our ideal balanced economy, taking into account the ideas of capitalism and its Darwin components such as the idea of "survival of the fittest", we would have an economic situation where most of society is in the middle; "The middle class". Then you have some people who rise above and some people who fall below. This tends to be the natural order of things.

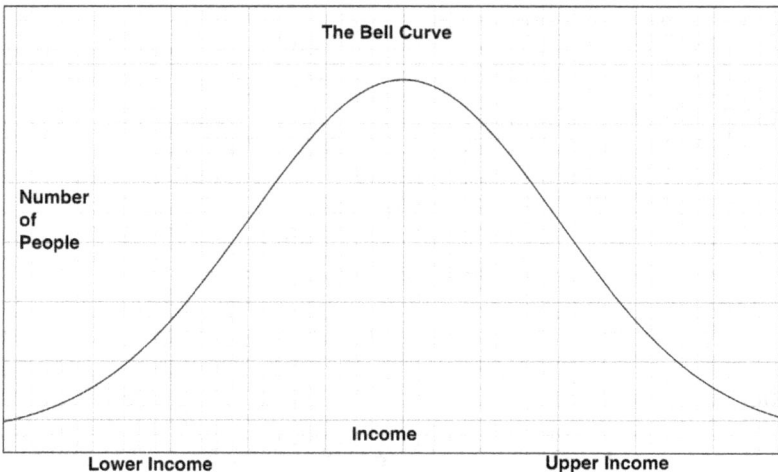

The bell curve, pictured in the graph above is a graphical representation of a natural phenomenon that we find in many aspects of our lives, science and nature. The bell curve shows that a majority of outcomes occur in the middle with fewer numbers above and below the average. I believe this is the outcome that best represents a balanced economy, where the majority of people can earn a decent living, where some can rise above the average and some may fall below.

Isn't this our ideal economic situation to strive for? Shouldn't we strive for a situation where a majority of Americans can do well for themselves? If it is the mandate of the U.S. government to ensure the welfare of its people, shouldn't it be the government's objective to obtain an income distribution as represented by the bell curve? In this ideal situation the Median Household Income represents the amount that the largest number of people in the middle of the bell curve makes. Then there are the few poor who fall below and the few wealthy who rise above the average.

Of course in a perfect world we would all be rich beyond our wildest dreams. (But we know that's not gonna happen.) First, it is natural that some people aren't willing to work as hard as others and so shouldn't achieve the same wealth and success if they didn't put in the same amount of effort. I do recognize and believe that this is a necessary and natural aspect of capitalism. We want to reward hard work and not those who would be lazy. Also, there simply aren't enough resources for the seven billion people on the planet to live a life of luxury. All seven billion living in the lap of luxury isn't physically possible.

Let's look at the graph of the bell curve on the following page, where the horizontal (x axis) represents income level and the vertical (y axis) represents the number of people at a certain income level. The center hump in the curve shows that most people's income would be in the middle. As the curve moves left of center, it shows a fewer number of people earning less. As we move to the right of center, some people are able to do much better.

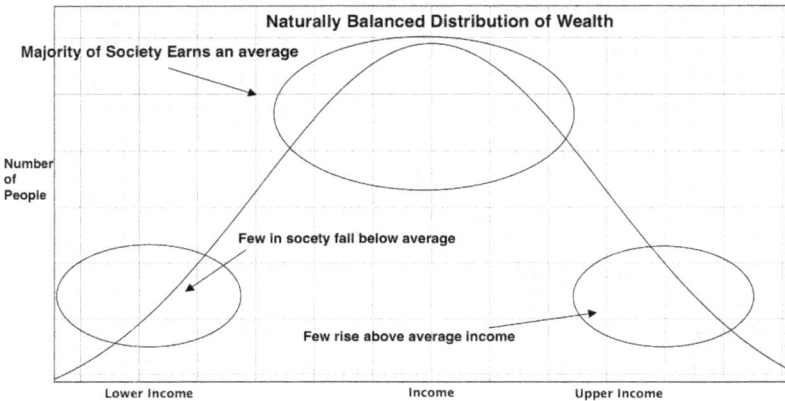

Naturally Balanced Distribution of Wealth

Majority of Society Earns an average

Number of People

Few in socety fall below average

Few rise above average income

Lower Income   Income   Upper Income

Now assuming we agree that the bell curve described is a natural order to things and an economic situation that we hope to obtain and sustain, we can now look again at GDP. As GDP grows, if our distribution of wealth according to the bell curve is to be maintained, then Median Household Income should increase as well at the same rate. The next table on the following page shows side by side our GDP per capita and MHI for every 5 years. I also list their rates of increase or decrease over those periods. (GDP per capita is the amount each person would earn if GDP were divided evenly among the population. We use GDP per capita in order to take into account population changes as it relates to overall GDP)

By looking at the table below we can see there has been a definite trend over the past 50 years and it isn't a pleasant one, not for the majority of Americans. From 1960 to present, our GDP per capita has grown consistently. If we do the math GDP per capita has grown 126% since 1960. Remember GDP per capita is an average. So, if the average GDP per person has increased 126% and we are trying to maintain a balance of wealth, then the Median Household Income, which represents the people in the middle of our bell curve should have increased as well by 126%.

68

Year	Gross Domestic Product/capita	GDP Rate of change	Median Household Income	MHI Rate of change
1960	$21,260		$39,850	
1965	$25,415	+19.5%	$45,553	+14.3%
1970	$28,143	+10.7%	$49,148	+7.9%
1975	$30,528	+8.5%	$42,936	-14.4%
1980	$32,304	+5.8%	$44,059	2.6%
1985	$35,729	+10.6%	$45,069	2.3%
1990	$38,546	+7.9%	$47,818	6.1%
1995	$39,522	+2.5%	$47,803	-.01%
2000	$43,898	+11.1%	$52,500	9.8%
2005	$46,789	+6.6%	$51,093	-2.8%
2010	$47,988	+2.5%	$49,777	-2.6%

All numbers adjusted for 2010 inflation[xii]

Unfortunately this is not the case. We do the math and find that Median Household Income has only increased a measly 25%. A majority of people only earned 25% more versus an average growth of 126%. In this situation we can see what has happened to our balanced bell curve over time. The graph below shows what happens as GDP per capita grows substantially faster than the MHI.

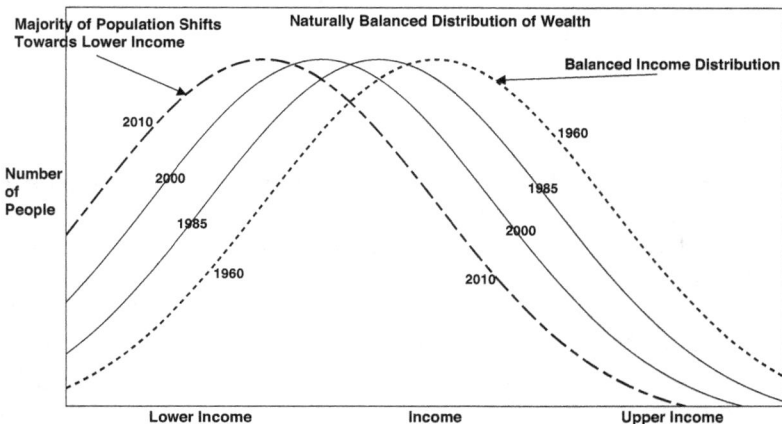

Looking at this graph we can see, based on the historical numbers of GDP per-capita and MHI that the greatest number of people in the middle of our bell curve has shifted to the left or lower income side. This is a perfect depiction of what has been happening. "The rich getting richer and the poor getting poorer." These are the numbers. These are the facts!

Look again at the graph on the previous page and the trend that has been occurring. Ask yourself; how can this trend continue? The answer is that it cannot continue forever. A continuing trend like this will eventually lead to mass poverty, high crime, high inflation and an utter collapse of society. As we mentioned before concerning the French Revolution, whenever there is mass poverty you cannot have a stable society as uprisings and revolutions are sure to occur.

Does this trend that we have seen represent a shift towards socialist ideals? No, the exact opposite has been occurring. A shift towards extreme socialist ideals would show everyone in society starting to earn the same amount, which is clearly not happening. Instead we have a growing income gap and a decreasing shift of the Median income over the past 50 years.

Now that we have seen the trends and relationships between GDP and MHI, next we need to look at our tax rates since 1960. In doing this we can see how increases or decreases in tax rates may have affected the relationship between GDP versus Median Household Income.

Taxes: Sustaining The Great Divide

We have clearly established a trend occurring where more and more people are earning less and less as compared to GDP. First, we have to ask ourselves if this a good thing? Is our government fulfilling its mandate to promote the general welfare and ensure liberty if there is an undeniable trend where the majority of its citizens continuously earn lower and lower wages then the average?

There may be many factors that allow this trend to continue. But one of the biggest contributing factors is our tax structure. Of course no one likes paying taxes, but in a civil society the government needs to be funded somehow.

How much overall revenue does the government need to generate? The government provides services to its citizens, services that need to be paid for. This relates back to the issue concerning the overall "size" of government, which was addressed in Chapter 1. Once we have established how much revenue the government needs to generate from taxes, the next question is, who should pay taxes and how much do we each pay?

The question of "who should pay?" is an easy answer I think we would all agree with. In a civil democracy, where everyone lives freely and gets a chance to vote, everyone should be monetarily responsible for the functions and services that the government supplies. Then the debate arises, "how much or what percentage should people pay?" Extreme conservatives argue that everyone should pay exactly the same amount, which is often called "The Flat Tax". Republicans who have proposed the Flat Tax believe everyone, regardless of how much they earn should pay an equal share. Sounds fair right?

To find an answer to the question "how much people should pay?" let's first look at what tax rates have been in the past. We do this to see if there is a relationship between tax rates and the trend of growing income disparity.

The next chart below shows what the tax rates were for people in the upper and lower tax brackets. Listed are the rates for someone earning in the lower percentile, around $36K per year in 2010, with equivalent amounts adjusted for inflation during previous years. Then I show tax rates for the higher percentile of income earners at $250K and their equivalent amounts adjusted for inflation. As an example, today's $250,000 is equal to $33,900 back in 1960 when adjusted for inflation. The tax rate for someone earning a very respectable $33,900 in 1960 was 65%. (Tax rates used are for single filers.)

After taking tax rates from the upper and lower income earners, we divide these numbers into each other and come up with what I call a "Tax Disparity Coefficient" or ratio. For example, by using tax rates from the 1960s, which was 65% (upper tax rate) divided by 26% (the lower tax rate) we come up with a number: 2.5 in this case. This number represents how equal (or unequal) the tax rates were between the lower and upper income earners. If both

71

groups were paying the same rate, as happened in 1990, the Tax Disparity Coefficient is 1. 1 represents equal tax rates for everyone. As the coefficient moves higher than 1, the further the gap grows between tax rates for the upper and lower income brackets.

Year	36K/year Adjusted for inflation	Lower Income tax rate	250K/year Adjusted for inflation	Upper Income tax rate	Tax Disparity Coefficient	Rate of change as a %
1960	$4,900	26%	$33,900	65%	2.5	
1965	$5,200	22%	$36,000	55%	2.5	0%
1970	$6,400	25%	$44,400	60%	2.4	-4.2%
1975	$8,900	25%	$61,600	64%	2.56	+6.7%
1980	$13,600	26%	$94,300	68%	2.62	+2.3%
1985	$17,700	23%	$123,100	50%	2.17	-21%
1990	$21,500	28%	$149,600	28%	1	-117%
1995	$25,100	28%	$174,400	36%	1.29	+29%
2000	$28,400	28%	$197,100	36%	1.29	0%
2005	$32,190	25%	$223,550	33%	1.14	-13%
2010	$36,000	25%	$250,000	33%	1.14	0%

xiii

Now that we have this Tax Disparity Coefficient, we can then find out a rate of change. How much as a percentage did the tax code move towards or away from a situation where everyone is paying an equal percentage of taxes?

Finally we can take this rate of change in our tax code, put it alongside our previous figures concerning the rate of change in Median Household Income and see if there is a correlation between the two.

When we do this as shown in the graph on the following page, there seems to be a consistent correlation. 5-year periods that saw tax rates get closer or more even between the upper and lower income earners were followed by periods where Median Household Income drops. The opposite is true as well. When the gap between tax-rates increased, periods followed where the growth rate for Median Household Income had risen.

MHI Change VS. Tax Disparity Change

MHI rate change   Tax Disparity

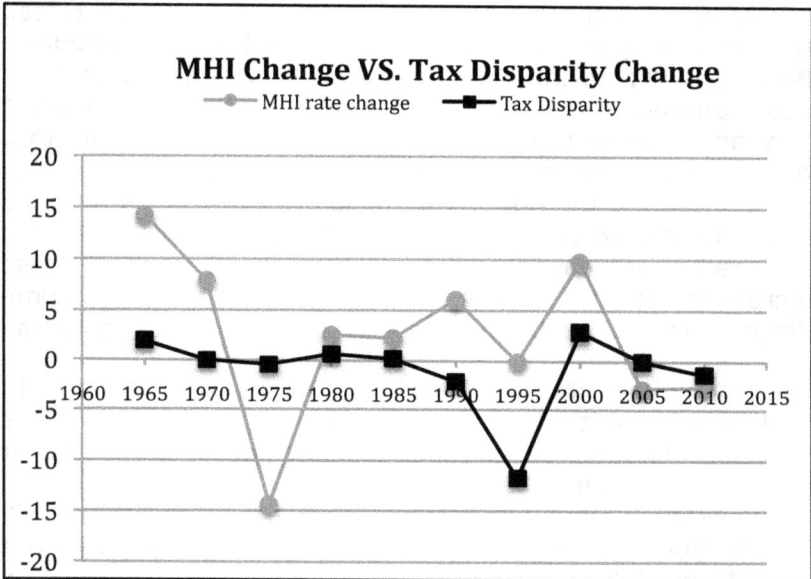

The first telling point of this graph is between 1965-1970, where the gap between tax rates shrunk, changing the tax disparity by -4.6%. Tax rates moved closer towards people with upper and lower incomes paying the same rate. This was followed by a period between 1970-1975 where Median Household income dropped by 14.4%. Next was 1970-1980, where taxes on the wealthy were raised by 9% over this ten-year period. Shortly after, starting in 1975-1985 Median Household income grew 5.9%. Then the next startling correlation is the Reagan and Bush Senior years 1980-1992. Here we see the gap in tax rates drop by over 130%, where both low and high-income earners were paying the same percentage of tax. After these equal tax rates were implemented, Household Median Income dropped again shortly after. We went from a previous increase of 6.1% between 1985-1990, to decreasing 6 percentage points from 1990 to 1995. The next big change in tax code came under Bill Clinton where he raised taxes on the upper income brackets, increasing the rate gap between tax brackets from 1992 to 1995. Our data shows us the 5-year period that followed from 1995-2000 saw a huge jump in Median Household income of 9.8%. And finally we had the Bush Jr. years, during which he closed the tax rate gap again by 13% over his term as president. Between 2000 to 2005 MHI dropped by 2.8% and dropped again another 2.6% from 2005 to 2010. Median Household Income reversed from a steady increase in prior years to a total drop of 5.4% during the Bush presidency.

These are the numbers. These are the facts. There is a clear undeniable correlation, which shows that as the gap in tax rates increased, Median Household Income also increased. It also shows that Median Household income drops when income brackets pay closer to the same tax rate.

Of course the relationship of individual tax rates to MHI is only part of the story in a complicated economic system. Another major factor to include is corporate or business tax rates.

Below is hopefully the last big table of numbers I will burden you with. But it is a necessary and very important piece to our tax puzzle.

Year	Individual Tax Revenue	Corporate Tax Revenue	Total Tax Revenue	Corporate Revenue as a % of total
1960	$40,715	$21,494	$62,209	34.5%
1965	$48,792	$25,461	$74,253	34.3%
1970	$90,412	$32,829	$123,241	26.6%
1975	$122,386	$40,621	$163,007	24.9%
1980	$244,069	$64,600	$308,669	20.9%
1985	$334,531	$61,331	$395,862	15.5%
1990	$466,884	$93,507	$560,391	16.6%
1995	$590,244	$157,004	$747,248	21.0%
2000	$1,004,462	$207,289	$1,211,751	17.1%
2005	$927,222	$278,282	$1,205,504	23.0%
2010	$935,771	$156,741	$1,092,512	14.3%

Numbers in Billions of Dollars[xiv]

This table shows the actual tax revenue generated by individuals and by corporations over the past 50 years. Then in the last column I figured what percentage of tax revenue was generated by businesses. We can see that in

1960 corporations generated 34.5% of government tax revenue. Then look at the current figures where corporations only contributed 14.3% in 2010. The inverse of this means that individuals used to contribute 65.5% of tax revenue 50 years ago and now are supplying 85.7% of federal tax revenue.

So, if GDP has steadily increased and Median Household income has remained stagnant or actually decreased, how is it possible that corporations who used to contribute 34% of overall tax revenue now only contribute 14% of revenue? Especially if we have fairly high corporate tax rates, shouldn't corporations be generating more in tax revenue, and why not?

One answer is "Loopholes". Loopholes are rules in our tax code or legal technicalities, which allow big businesses to avoid paying their fair share or what they are supposed to pay. The biggest loophole is where corporations keep money in overseas accounts, enabling them to avoid paying taxes. Adding to the lost revenue from loopholes is numerous other laws that allow corporations to pay rates lower than the standard corporate rate. There is the Accelerated Depreciation Deduction that allows companies to deduct the depreciation of investments as well as interest paid on those investments at the same time. Then there are deductions for shipping jobs overseas in the form of moving expenses when companies ship operations overseas.

The result is larger profits for big business and a bigger tax burden required of individuals and small businesses. Small businesses end up having to pay the higher corporate tax rate because they don't have the same resources to work around loopholes that the multinational companies have; things like keeping money in overseas accounts.

Just the fortune 500 companies alone are able to avoid paying billions upon billions of tax revenue legally through these loopholes. The top corporate tax rate in the U.S. now is 35%. Exxon Mobile paid only 13% on 41 billion dollars in profit.[xv] GE paid 7.4% on 14 billion. And Apple's effective tax rate was 9.8%, paying 2.4 Billion less then it should have.[xvi] These are just 3 companies that collectively cost our government (and us) over 15 billion dollars in one year. Remember these are just three companies I've listed. Hundreds more use the same tactics to avoid paying U.S.

taxes. These companies are able to do this by keeping profits in overseas accounts in countries such as the Netherlands, Luxembourg and the Cayman and British Virgin Islands. So, if GDP is growing as a result of the money generated by these companies, why are they paying a lower percentage of overall tax revenue? The result is a larger tax burden on individuals and small businesses.

In the U.S. we have some of the lowest individual tax rates in the world. And if we look at comparisons to other countries, we do have a fairly high corporate tax rate, which should and can be lowered. If we were to close these loopholes for the large corporations, allowing us to generate more revenue, then the overall tax rates on all businesses can be lowered, without negatively affecting revenue. While lowering the tax rate can be a great incentive to attract foreign business and help our own small businesses, the trend of increased tax burdens on individuals has not changed. These loopholes must be closed before there can be any real discussion about what actual tax rates are fair and advantageous to the people and businesses, big and small. Especially considering those hard-line conservatives who argue, "corporations are people too" and want corporations to have equal rights as individuals. Shouldn't they be subjected to the same tax laws that individual citizens have to abide by, including paying tax on foreign profits?

Capital Gains Tax: A Loophole for Individuals.

Just as loopholes need to be closed down for corporations so there can be low competitive tax rates for all businesses without drastically affecting tax revenues, the same idea can be applied to Capital Gains, which is in essence a loophole for individuals. Capital Gains, for the many of us who don't know, is a separate classification of income. It is investment income taxed at a lower rate than normal income, 0% for some up to 15% for most. Capital Gains pertains mostly to income that is earned by investments, including interest earned from holding stocks, bonds, mutual funds, etc. It is income that is earned by you; where you do nothing other than invest your money. I like to call it "unearned income" since you didn't really have anything directly to do with earning the money. (I will address for those who invest as their primary job in a moment). Just as big businesses use tax loopholes to pay a lower effective tax rate, individuals who earn a large portion of their income from investments, also are allowed to pay a substantially lower effective tax rate.

The biggest argument used by conservatives in-favor of low capital gains tax rates, is that they say it affects most Americans. Capital Gains do affect most Americans regarding two aspects of our lives. First, any profit earned from the sale of a house is taxed under the lower capital gains rate. Most people, especially the middle class do not pay tax when they sell their home because they don't make enough profit on it. Most people sell their home to buy another one. When you use the money from selling your house to buy a new one, you no longer need to pay any tax on that sale. If people say low capital gains rates are needed because it's a tax on peoples homes, this effects only the wealthy who actually profit from selling large homes and people who have multiple homes. Any profit from selling a second home is classified under capital gains. How many of you actually fit into this category?

The other argument used to continue our country's low capital gains rate is that it effects people's retirement investments. This is 100% true, which is why we can reclassify retirement investments separately from other capital gains. Currently people are encouraged to invest and save for retirement by offering tax deferred retirement accounts. We want people to invest for retirement. It helps move the economy and enables our senior citizens to financially care for themselves. This is why we have tax-deferred IRAs, Roth accounts, 401Ks, etc. But these avenues for saving are still fairly limited. Most people are only allowed to contribute $5000 per year into IRA accounts. If you wish to save and invest more then the allowed limit, you have to open your own personal savings and investment accounts, which are taxed under capital gains. We can continue to grow and improve people's savings by increasing limits and opportunities for tax-deferred retirement savings. Retirement savings could have their own classification of income, which is not taxed at all or taxed very low.

But the biggest beneficiary of low capital gains tax is

the wealthy. It is what allows people who have significant investment income to pay lower effective tax rates then middle class Americans. The upper class has large amounts of disposable income tied up in investments. They are able to earn exponentially more money without actually doing any work, which is why I call it "unearned income". It is what allows someone like Warren Buffet to pay a lower percentage on his income than his middle class secretary who pays a higher percentage. How does this work? Here is an example:

In the chart below we have Joe who is the CEO of a major corporation that pays him 1 million dollars a year plus 10 million in stock options. He has saved up and invested an additional 50 million dollars of his own, where he earned 6 million dollars in returns. Between both his job and his investment returns he earned 7 million dollars, paid 1.25 million dollars in taxes, which works out to be only 17.8% of his income.

	Income	Tax Rate	Tax owed in dollars
Joe	Earns 1 million dollars from job, taxed as individual income.	35%	$350,000
	60 million in investments, which earns 10% interest or 6 million dollars taxed as Capital Gains.	15%	$900,000
	Earned a total of 7 million for the year.	**17.8%**	$1.25 mil
Lydia	Earns 40k as a school teacher, taxed as individual income.	**25%**	$10,000

Lydia is a middle class schoolteacher who only earns 40 thousand dollars a year. She pays a supposed lower tax rate of 25%, but Joe is actually paying a smaller percentage of 17.8% on money he earned mostly from investing. Is this fair? Just because you have money and can write a check to an investment bank to invest your money, allows you to pay a lower tax rate on your income. But if you don't have money to spare, you have to pay a higher tax rate on the money you physically work to earn. How can anyone argue that this is fair or rational?

Then there are those for whom investing is their primary job and or business. If this is the case you should be able to choose and elect investment returns as individual income, where it is taxed at the same rate as everyone else's income or you can treat it as a business and be taxed as a business. If you run your investments as a business then you can pay yourself a salary where you are taxed at regular individual income rates. On top of this, you can have regular tax-deferred retirement savings just like everyone else. But to have a special lower rate just because you are an investor doesn't seem to make sense.

One can argue that because of low capital gains we have had such a boom in investing, where everyone wants to just be an investor. No one wants to actually work or produce tangible things that are really worth anything anymore. You can't have a society of nothing but investors and no one producing anything. Some economists argue that this trend of investing vs. producing was a key factor contributing to our economic meltdown in 2007. People will say it was the housing industry. The housing industry was part of the cause, but it really was the investment business that played a big part. We've had too much investing and nothing produced to back it up.[xvii]

Most of us want to invest and we should all be able to invest if we can, especially for retirement. The government should and can further encourage this behavior by expanding tax-free retirement accounts. But continuing to allow some to pay less tax and hence earn exponentially more money just because they have the money to invest seems backwards. It is these lower tax rates on things such as capital gains that directly contribute to the growing gap in wealth disparity. It is a policy of giving more to those who already have and punishing those who don't.

In conclusion, when it comes to taxes we can argue whether big businesses should pay a higher or lower tax rate. But first we need to begin by making sure big businesses are paying their fair share by closing loopholes. We can have arguments asking if the wealthy should pay a higher rate or the same rate. But we should first start by not allowing the wealthy to pay a lower rate than the working middle class. This has been happening due to the separate capital gains tax. We can argue about what tax rates are best for the economy and what best promotes job growth. Will a tax break here create more jobs or will tax breaks there encourage people to spend? (More on "Job Creators" in Chapter 8.) Most importantly though, we can start by being fair and not giving preferential treatment to some people just because they have money to invest, allowing them to pay a lower rate.

Taxes and Morality

There is one last bit I would like to address about taxes and tax rates. Some will argue that to be fair we should just pay the same dollar amount, say $10,000 for example. Why don't we all just pay $10k each and call it a day?

Everyone should pay something. And everyone does pay something unless you are a hermit living in the woods. Even the poor who may pay no income tax, still buys gas and other things that they pay tax on. (We address this further in the next section)

The main question is why should the wealthy pay more or a higher percentage than others? As we discussed earlier, progressive tax rates help to sustain a middle class that is needed for a healthy economy. But here is another answer for those who would ask "Isn't it fair to pay the same rate?" Well, no and here is why.

Earning money is exponential! One simple phrase comes to mind; "It takes money to make money". In other words, the more money you have the more money you can make. If everyone invested their money and saw a 10% return on their investment, the average person who was able to save $1000 would earn $100 on their savings at 10%. The wealthy person who has done well and was able to save and invest 10 million dollars would earn an additional 1 million dollars over the same period. So two people did the same thing. They both invested their savings and earned a 10% return. The average person made $100 and the wealthy person made $1,000,000. They both did the same investing, yet the person who had money was able to make a whole lot more, <u>10,000 times more</u> by doing the same investing, putting in the same amount of effort. If someone can earn 10 thousand times more money just because they already had money, is it wrong for them to pay a higher percentage of tax on those earnings?

I know many will say it's not right to punish people for doing well. And I agree we shouldn't punish those who do well. But is it a punishment, asking those who have done so well because of the system to give back a bit more in order to ensure the system still works for everyone in the future? In our previous example, we could ask the average person who earned $100 from investment income to pay 10% in taxes, which would leave them with $90 left after taxes.   The person who earned $1,000,000 from an investment could pay double that, even triple like 30%, leaving them with $666,666. That is still a lot of money to have earned from investing.

Which brings us to another argument used against taxing the wealthy at higher rates. The GOP will say taxation stifles the motivation to invest and make money. They say "why should I work or earn money if I just have to give it to the government?" This may be true if tax rates were above 50%. But does a tax increase from 15% to 30% make people not want to earn money? Of course not! Even taxed at 30% the investor in the above example was still able to walk away with an extra $666,666. Who would say at a 30% tax rate, "I don't want to make money anymore if I have to give some of it to the government"?

One other point needs to be addressed towards the defenders of low tax rates for the wealthy, who call raising taxes an unfair punishment on the affluent. It's not a punishment if there is a clear goal of using the tax code to help sustain a vibrant middle class, which is not only good for the overall country but is also needed in order for the wealthy to continue to do well. It's pretty simple; no middle class equals no growing economy and no one's businesses will do well.   Henry Ford, the founder of Ford Motor Company understood the need to preserve the middle class all too well. He said in order for his company to prosper, his workers (i.e.; the middle class) need to earn a living where they could afford to buy his product.

Let's not forget as part of society we all have our obligations and responsibilities towards that society in which we live. Our country has been set-up and organized so that people can prosper, which is what we all want. If you do well because of the system it should be your responsibility to help ensure that those who follow behind still have the same opportunities to prosper as you have. In order for others to do well in the future we still need infrastructure, education, safety and security for all, which is paid for with taxes!

Who Pays Taxes? The 50% Republican Spin

There is a statement being used in politics today by the GOP as an argument against raising taxes on the wealthy. You may have heard GOP members use the statement "Only 50% of Americans pay income taxes and the other 50% doesn't pay any income taxes". While there is some truth to this statement, it is a grossly simplified remark designed to make the public think that the top half of America is fully supporting and already paying for the bottom 50%, which is simply not true. Let's break it all down.

Yes it is true that only half of Americans pay federal income tax. But if you look at all federal tax revenue, which was 2.2 trillion dollars in 2010, only 42% of all federal revenue came from income taxes. The other 58% of tax revenue comes from other sources. 40% comes from payroll taxes. Everyone who works, no matter how much or little earned contributes to payroll tax revenue.

It is these payroll taxes that directly pay for programs such as Social Security and Medicare. Everyone contributes 4.2% on the first $106,800 they earn towards Social Security and another 1.45% for Medicare.[*] So this means that someone who earns 40K a year pays a higher percentage of their income in payroll taxes than a person who earns 1 million a year. The person that earns a million dollars only pays the 4.2% on the first $106,800, which works out to be a minuscule amount compared to their overall income.

So, all workers have been paying these taxes and

---

[*] Figures listed are the employee's contribution to Social Security and Medicare. Employers pay an additional 6.2% and 1.45% respectively into these programs. Self - employed individuals pay the combined employee and employer portions of 10.4% for Social Security and 2.9% for Medicare.

paying for their own Social Security and Medicare benefits. In fact, the surpluses from these taxes have been used to help fund other areas of government. We will go into more detail on the Social Security conundrum in the next chapter. For now just understand that everyone, not just the top 50% pay these payroll taxes.

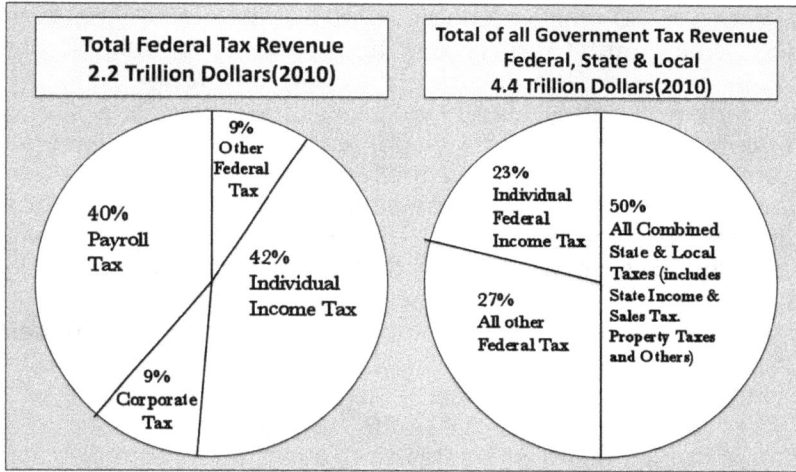

**Total Federal Tax Revenue
2.2 Trillion Dollars(2010)**

9% Other Federal Tax

40% Payroll Tax

42% Individual Income Tax

9% Corporate Tax

**Total of all Government Tax Revenue
Federal, State & Local
4.4 Trillion Dollars(2010)**

23% Individual Federal Income Tax

50% All Combined State & Local Taxes (includes State Income & Sales Tax, Property Taxes and Others)

27% All other Federal Tax

xviii   xix

Then there is a whole other source of tax revenue that the "Fifty Percenters" are leaving out: State and local taxes. Everybody who owns a home pays property taxes and anyone who purchases anything pays sales taxes. Then there are other taxes in the form of fees for things such as driver's licenses, deeds of trust and gas taxes. Figure in all of these things and the bottom 50% pay a much higher share of their income towards these taxes than anyone else.

If you add all tax revenue collected by federal, state and local governments in 2010, it comes to about 4.4 trillion dollars. Of the total 4.4 trillion collected, federal income taxes accounted for only 23% of total revenue. So while it may be true that the top 50% of Americans pay most of the federal income tax, there is still another 77% of government revenue, which is paid by everyone.

Next we can take a deeper look into why only 50% of Americans pay income tax. Who is the other 50% that the

GOP say don't pay their fair share?   Out of a total 310 million people in the U.S. there are about 60 million children below the age of 16. There are 20 million young adults in college or other schooling who don't work full time.   We have about 40 million seniors, most of who live on fixed incomes and have already paid their income taxes for the previous 40 years of their working lives.   And finally we have about 30 million people who live below the poverty line.   Well, right there is just about the other half of the population. Even though they may not pay federal income tax, remember they all pay taxes in other ways and spend an overwhelmingly higher percentage of their overall income on these taxes. All these people buy things, which they pay sales tax on. All the seniors who own their homes still pay property taxes.   All the college students still pay gas taxes to drive and even if they have part time jobs, still pay payroll taxes for Social Security and Medicare.

As an example, take a low-income earner who makes $30,000 a year before taxes. They will still pay 6.65% in Social Security and Medicare taxes. (9.1% if self-employed) If that person spends $12,000 on goods, services and utilities subjected to 5% sales tax (average combined state and local rates are much higher), they pay $600 in sales taxes. If they own a small home they may pay about $800 in property taxes, then add any other fees, gas taxes etc. All together, even if this person didn't pay any federal income tax, they still spent about 14% of their income on taxes.

Now anytime you hear someone say, "Only 50% of Americans pay income tax" you can see through this statement as an attempt to make you think only the top 50 percent supports everyone else, which is clearly false.

Chapter 7
Current Problems and Arguments

Class Warfare

Recently in the political arena there has been a loud scream from the right anytime there is talk of raising taxes on the wealthy. They scream, "Class warfare!" Anytime in the past few years that the administration has suggested raising taxes, John Boehner the Republican leader of the House was on the frontlines calling any such move to raise taxes on the wealthy a sign of class warfare.[xx] My question here is: Who started the war?

Over the past few years, anytime someone on the left proposes raising taxes on the wealthy, Republicans try to convince the public that this is class warfare and a punishment on the rich. Is trying to get the wealthy to pay their fair share, when they enjoy numerous tax breaks and a low 15% rate on capital gains so much a war on the rich? If the wealthy pay effective tax rates that are lower than rates for middle class Americans, is asking the wealthy to at least pay the same rate class warfare? What if we were to show that increased taxes on the wealthy are a clear means to grow the economy and not so much a punishment as some would claim?

One could easily look at the history of our tax code and be more correct by saying that tax breaks given to the wealthy, implemented over the past 30 years was class warfare engaged by the affluent against the middle class and poor. Tax rates for the wealthy are already the lowest they have been in 80 years. (See chart on next page) Now the 99% are simply trying to fight back.

The affluent have had the resources to lobby and influence tax policy in their favor, reducing their effective tax rates significantly. This is what allows the top 1% to acquire a greater share of the country's wealth. We were all told that these tax policies were enacted to spur investment and job creation. But, relying solely on "trickle down theory" is not a formula for building the economy. As we have seen recently, the latest recession and job losses occurred while

85

operating under a policy where the wealthy have enjoyed the lowest tax rates in generations.

History of Top Tax Rates

Year	Rate	Bracket (earning over) Married filing Jointly
1917	67%	$2,000,000
1920	73%	$1,000,000
1923	58%	$200,000
1925-1931	25%	$100,000
1932	63%	$1,000,000
1936	79%	$5,000,000
1941	81%	$5,000,000
1942	88%	$200,000
1952	92%	$200,000
1958	91%	$400,000
1963-1976	70%	$200,000
1982	50%	$85,600
1987	38.5%	$90,000
1990	28%	$32,450
1993	39.6%	$250,000
2003	35%	$311,000

xxi

Let's look at the twenty-year period leading up to the recession from 1987-2007. Operating under lower tax rates for the wealthy during this period, which was supposed to spur the economy by way of "trickle down" theory, the top 1% saw their share of total Adjusted Gross Income (AGI) increase by 85%. What about the bottom 50%? Their share of the country's Adjusted Gross Income actually decreased 22%. Then add in factors of population growth, where the top 1% saw 349,000 tax filers added to their ranks over this twenty-year period. The bottom 50% of tax filers saw an increase of 17.4 million people added to this lower class. 17.4 million people were added to a class that made up 22% less of overall AGI. xxii

All this has happened while we continued to operate

under a system of lower tax rates for the wealthy. So much for "trickle down economics" actually trickling down.

If we want to end this trend of disproportionate wealth distribution and class warfare, then effective personal income tax rates for the wealthy should at least be the same as that of the middle class. Anytime someone on the right screams, "Class warfare!" ask them who started the war? Warren Buffett knows all too well who started the war. He has stated, "There's class warfare all right, but it's my class, the rich class that's making war, and we're winning."[xxiii]

Keep Your Gov't Hands Off Of My Medicare

There was an instance at a Tea Party rally in 2010, where a guy was holding up a sign that said "Keep Your Gov't Hands Off My Medicare".

Unfortunately it is obvious that this Tea partier didn't seem to understand that it is the government's hand that is giving him his Medicare. There has been a large movement from the extreme right against big government and anyone who is supposedly for "big government". The argument has gotten so out of control that many people seem to forget about those things the government does provide, which most of us benefit from.

The obvious areas of government spending that most people benefit from are education and defense. We are also protected by our police forces and fire departments. We all travel on roads that are paid for by the government. There are millions of seniors who do benefit from Medicare. Regrettably the aforementioned Tea partier seemed to forget who it is that supplies him with this benefit.

Then there are many other important government laws, regulations and programs that are just as important. Many in the Tea party seem to forget about things that actually support the Republican agenda of being pro-business. Carelessly using generalizations to speak out against all government regulations, without thinking and knowing those regulations that we benefit from, is no way to move forward in a positive discussion.

One of the most important pro-business growth

regulations that the government passed was the Bankruptcy Act in 1898, amended in 1938 and again in 1978. The Bankruptcy Act helps encourage business growth by minimizing people's financial risk when going into business. This law protects people and their businesses from creditors if the business fails. This law is one of the biggest contributors that encourage people to take risks and helps spawn new innovation and growth. If we were to take a position of true free-market policies then The Bankruptcy Act should be seen from the right as a horrible intrusion of government into the free-market. But this is one example of pro-business government interference in the free-market. It is a policy that has helped spur growth and innovation, which many people accidentally or purposefully forget about.

Standard of Living (by whose standards?)

We often hear politicians and pundits talk about America's high standard of living. It is true that America has one of the highest standards of living. But what does standard of living mean? While the definition can be a bit fuzzy, the main factors that relate to the term "standard of living" are things such as: Income per capita; access to material goods and mortality rates.

Most of the numbers used to describe the standard of living are figured as averages. So if there is a high-income disparity or a large gap between rich and poor, then averages won't give you an accurate representation of what is going on. I do not want to break apart the system that economists use to gauge standard of living, but wish to better define the factors we use to assess standard of living.

To determine our standard of living we normally look at the overall income level that the population earns. In 2010 the average household income was $49,445, just about the same as it was 20 years prior in 1989. But what about the factors it took to earn that income. Working 40 hours a week used to be the standard working week. Now many Americans are working 50, 60, 70, and even 80 hours a week in order to earn the same income. A study from Michael Greenstone and Adam Looney of the Brookings

Institute found that while American households may have increased their earnings by 23% since 1975 they are working 26% longer hours. They also report that most of the increase in household earnings was due to women working and earning more while men's wages remained stagnant or actually decreased.[xxiv] Does this trend of working longer hours represent an increased standard of living? While some work more in order to afford I-pads and Plasma TVs, which have become cheaper, the costs of housing and healthcare has risen substantially faster than the Median Household Income. Housing prices rose 39% above standard inflation rates from 1975-2009.[xxv] And healthcare costs have nearly doubled over the last ten years. As the cost of living increases, people's wages have remained stagnant.

Capitalism has capitalized on the value of human labor and demanded more for less. This is a direct result of competition with cheap foreign labor in a globalized world. To counteract this trend we have had labor unions, which will be discussed in the next section.

For now we should consider how the declining value of our own work affects the overall picture of America's standard of living. The value of our work has decreased and most people need to work more in order to earn the same amount so that they may pay their bills. It is figured that someone earning the minimum wage today is actually earning less than the equivalent worker in 1968. [xxvi]

When you consider access to material goods as a factor affecting our standard of living, the U.S. has been at the top. However with globalization many places around the world now have access to the same goods and services we do. The question of concern in a globalized world is no longer, "who doesn't have access to material goods?" but more importantly we should be asking who can and cannot afford these goods? The bigger the income gap becomes, the more and more people aren't able to afford goods and services, making access to them pointless. So if most people around the world now have access to certain goods and services, shouldn't we then focus on trying to make sure these goods are affordable? What about the affordability of necessities like medical care? Yes, America leads the world in having the latest and greatest healthcare technologies, medicines and procedures. But what good is it if only a small portion of the population can afford them? Can we really use our superior healthcare advances as a positive factor affecting our standard of living if people can't afford it? As of 2010, 16.3% of the U.S. population is uninsured making healthcare unaffordable for them.[xxvii] In the past twenty years 15 million people were added to the list of uninsured. Even though we may have advanced healthcare technology, it certainly cannot contribute positively to our country's overall standard of living when so many cannot afford it. This is why more and more people are traveling overseas to have medical procedures done at severely lower costs. In America, with a supposed high standard of living and great medical advances, Americans are traveling to India and South America to have major medical operations.

Unions and Collective Bargaining

Typically liberal Democrats support unions and conservative Republicans are against unions. This is a generalized statement that we use to label and categorize people's beliefs when it comes to unions. Republicans tend to see unions as a burden to business growth, an over-excessive expense to governments that hire public unions, and a strain on worker's freedom. Democrats view unions as a necessary way to organize support for workers rights. They believe unions are a means to combat powerful business interests.

This is one of those arguments where there are strong opinions on both sides. We need to take a step back in order to see that both sides are correct in their arguments. Both may have valid points but we can't just look at a few points on one side of the argument and make broad policy decisions for all. We have to look at the whole argument, the complete picture, if we are to come up with a workable, balanced solution concerning unions that is beneficial to everyone as a whole.

The recent debate has been brought about most notably due to the policies enacted by Republican Governor Scott Walker of Wisconsin, who passed a law limiting the collective bargaining rights of workers in public unions. In this debate, which sparked controversy throughout the country, there was a major flaw in Mr. Walker's arguments against collective bargaining. He tried to make it an issue concerning the state budget, saying that unions are a wasteful and excessive use of government funds. So, Governor Walker tried to enact laws against collective bargaining, using the excuse that it costs the state too much money, adding to the government's expenses and hence causing budget deficit problems.

The first problem with his argument is that there weren't budget problems because of inefficiencies in the unions. There were budget deficits because the state wasn't taking in much money from tax revenue and was wastefully spending it in other areas. Wisconsin's tax revenue went from steady increases to an -8.1% drop between 2007-2010.[xxviii] Wisconsin had one of the largest revenue losses out of any state during the recession. However, Mr. Walker wanted to target unions as the main reason for Wisconsin's budget woes. The point is that there still are services the state needs and someone has to handle and pay for them.

Soon after the debate in Wisconsin, other Republican led states tried enacting the same kind of laws against unions and collective bargaining, making it a national issue again. Republican governors and Republican led state legislators in Indiana, Arizona, Utah and Florida are just a few places that tried (some successfully, some unsuccessfully) to limit the collective bargaining rights of workers. Even in the U.S. Congress, the Republican led House passed a bill that proposed a 17% funding cut for the National Labor Relations Board (NLRB). The NLRB is the government organization that oversees elections for labor unions and investigates complaints of unfair labor practices. Cuts this large to the NLRB would mean that they could no longer effectively fill it's purpose of protecting workers as laid out in the 1935 National Labor Relations Act.

Instead of using unions as an excuse to curb budget deficits let us instead look at the positive and negative aspects that result from unions. First there have been some cases of waste and corruption within our country's unions, from embezzlements to bribes and the doctoring of false invoices. Many of these cases have been discovered and

91

prosecuted to the fullest extent of the law.[xxix] There are however ways to counteract these issues. One is coming up with standards, regulations and oversight of unions. Especially if it is a public union that works for the people, their financial books should be made public and clear in order to eliminate fraud.

Then there is the issue of laziness and proficiency. There are some workers who are overly protected by unions, which may encourage a culture of laziness. There are some teachers who are protected regardless of their performance. A survey from the Department of Education estimates that out of the teachers who received a "poor" grade, only 2.1% are dismissed.[xxx] While there may be some ineffective teachers, there are many more that are doing a great job educating our children. These few problems though can be dealt with. We can come up with fair standards and proficiency measures to counteract these issues. But it does not mean we should ban unions and collective bargaining altogether. Let's not forget why we have unions to begin with.

First, it is the right of the people to assemble as written in the first amendment to the Constitution. Everyone has the right to work, negotiate their salaries and if they want to, may do so collectively. There is nothing in the Constitution that could prevent this. And why do people choose to collectively bargain? What happened that spawned the birth of unions in the first place?

Unions were formed when the free-market capitalized and took advantage of people's lives and labor. Back in the 1800s into the early 1900s, with the industrial revolution picking up momentum, millions of people were working long hours in hazardous conditions for little pay. There are thousands of instances where people literally dropped dead from exhaustion, countless stories of people falling ill and dying due to bad ventilation in factories with hazardous materials, and a long list of other safety issues. People had to accept these working conditions in return for a low wage that enabled people to barely feed themselves. If they didn't like it, all they could do was accept it or quit and starve. It wasn't until the people collectively organized to demand higher pay, safer work environments, and reasonable breaks that things started to change.

Without unions the overall price of labor for the entire workforce would drop to levels that the average worker couldn't reasonably live off of. Companies wouldn't care to spend money to initiate safety measures on their own. Any demands that a company would make of its workers, such as working long hours or any other practices would only give the worker one recourse, quit or get fired. Then the only choice for the worker would be to go to another company that adheres solely to the same capitalistic principles of profit. Also, higher wages for workers means higher tax revenue for everyone. Remember that union workers, even public union workers still pay tax on their income. Higher wages also means more people buying things, which is good for businesses.

Most importantly we mustn't forget the atrocities that occurred in our factories during the turn of the last century. We must remember the times of low wages, child labor and unsafe working conditions. An elimination of unions would leave businesses free to return to these old practices, which would negatively affect all workers, even those who don't belong to unions. Yes, there are a few examples of fraud, corruption and waste, so let's work to fix these problems where they occur. But it doesn't mean that workers should be without any means for recourse to protect their own interests. And it certainly doesn't mean that just because a state has budget issues, that workers should be denied the right to collectively bargain in order to protect their own well being.

Pledges and Compromise, what does it mean?

A recent tactic used by extreme conservatives has been the adoption of pledges. One example is the pledge put forth by the right wing group Americans for Tax Reform, which states that members who sign this pledge promise to never raise taxes, no matter what! Almost all Republican congressmen have signed it and therefore have pledged to never raise taxes.[xxxi]

My question for these Republicans would be "Is there any point at which you would see a need and agree to raise taxes?" Let's suppose we put the tax rate to zero for a year. After which would you still pledge to not raise taxes? At what point would you see a need to raise taxes?

The problem with pledges like this one is that it does not allow or leave any room for compromise. It is an all or nothing strategy that has taken the GOP further to the right then ever. Even among their own ranks, if you haven't signed these pledges, then your peers assume you don't stand with them and are ousted from ever getting a chance to serve as a moderate Republican. Moderate Republicans serving in Congress are a dying breed. Of the 27 congressmen considered to be moderate Republicans in 2007, conservative Tea partiers defeated 11 of them. Nine of them retired, two switched parties and only five remain in office. xxxii

It's not hard to see how a growing number of extreme Republicans standing by pledges, such as the Tax pledge make any kind of compromise hard or almost impossible.

The National Debt

We all know that America has a huge national debt and large budget deficit. For those of you who don't understand the difference between debt and deficit: The national debt is our total bill; the total amount of money we currently owe as a country. Our deficit refers to the amount of money we are short on a yearly basis. The deficit is the difference in the amount of money we spend verses the amount of tax revenue collected by the government each year.

Our overall debt is around 14 trillion now, with no sign of shrinking. Few could deny that this is a huge problem. Due to our large debt the United State's credit rating has recently been downgraded. Why is our credit rating so important? We need to keep a good credit rating in order to attract investments into our country and our businesses.

Both Democrats and Republicans over the past 12 years are equally to blame for this looming issue. The biggest factors contributing towards this huge debt has been the Bush Tax Cuts, decreasing government revenue, the wars in Iraq and Afghanistan, the expansion of Medicare and Medicaid with rising healthcare costs, and the two large stimulus/bailout bills after the Great Recession hit in 2007. (We will focus on the specifics behind each of these issues individually in following sections.)

Focusing on the debt as a whole, the only way we can begin to solve this problem is by recognizing we are all to blame and that we all need to give in or give something up. It is the "all of the above" strategy that Barack Obama has spoken of, regarding the need to raise taxes and cut spending at the same time. However our highly polarized Congress can't seem to come to any kind of consensus.

First, cuts need to be made but done so in a smart manner. Defense and Medicaid are the two areas that will suffer most if any serious deficit reduction is to be made. These two programs are our government's largest expenditures. While cuts need to be made in these two areas as well as some others, we need to recognize areas of spending that are needed for America's future and growth; education, infrastructure and R&D! If we are to have a chance competing in the global economy, these areas need to be funded and more!

Cuts need to be made but we simply can't drastically cut budgets and expect prosperity. Items such as education and infrastructure are things we need and shouldn't be slashing if we want to prosper. (More on the importance of education, infrastructure and R&D explained in Chapters 8 and 9) While cuts are being made taxes will need to increase as well. We not only have some of the lowest tax rates in our history but we have enjoyed these low rates while at war. Throughout our history, whenever our country was at war taxes went up. When we went into Iraq and Afghanistan taxes didn't go up, we cut them! And now it is time to pay for it! We can do this by raising capital gains, closing corporate loopholes, eliminating certain deductions and raising rates in a fair and balanced fashion.

For too long our nation has had our cake for free and now its time to pay. Many individuals and companies have directly benefited financially from the three main contributors to our national debt. The companies of Kellogg Brown & Root, and Halliburton each received billions in taxpayer funded contracts.[xxxiii] The Iraq War that the American taxpayer is obligated to pay for, opened up oil markets that Exxon Mobile and other companies are now able to profit from. Then the first bailout package or TARP program benefited the companies of AIG, Bank of America, JP Morgan and Goldman Sachs. (There is a long list of other TARP beneficiaries) Even though these companies are supposed to pay back these borrowed funds, they still benefited by being able to stay in business, allowing them to later turn a profit.

It should only be fair that those who have benefited the most from this government spending, which contributes to our national debt, pay a portion of taxes congruent with the benefits they have received over the last decade.

Lost Revenue, The Bush Tax Cuts, and other Fiscal Irresponsibility

Back in the 1990s things were looking up for our country and our fiscal house. We had a balanced budget with yearly surpluses that could have been used to pay down our debt. Around that time our total debt was about five trillion dollars.[xxxiv] Bill Clinton accomplished this by making cuts in certain areas, most notably defense spending which is our number one government outlay. The other part of fiscal policy in the 90s that allowed us to have a balanced budget was our revenues. The government was taking in enough tax dollars to cover our expenses. So what happened?

While our current fiscal problem cannot be attributed to one thing alone, there were a few major policies enacted in the 2000s, turning our fiscal house upside down. The biggest problem was the Bush tax cuts! Not only did he cut taxes for future years, he also retroactively cut taxes for past years by sending out tax refund checks. Only people who paid federal income tax in 2000 got checks. Single filers got $300 each and married couples got $600. Another provision of the Bush tax cuts was that he lowered income tax rates by 3% for most people and 4.6% for the top earners. It also lowered the top capital gains tax rate to 15%.

Today we are debating the effects that the Bush tax cuts have had. To counteract the effects of these tax cuts the Buffet Rule was presented, proposed by multi-billionaire

Warren Buffet. Buffet has said that the top 1% who currently pay effective rates lower than middle class Americans should be paying at least the same percentage as the middle class.[xxxv] Republicans have argued that raising taxes on the wealthy would only account for a small portion of tax revenue and deficit reduction. This may have been the case with the recent proposal for the "Buffet Tax", which was a poorly written piece of legislation that didn't go far enough to fulfill what Warren Buffet was really proposing. The recent bill proposed in April of 2012, only asked for those who earn over 1 million dollars to pay a minimum of 30%. But the actual tax rate is 35% for everyone earning over $312,000. So, the proposed Buffet Tax would have only recovered a portion of the revenue lost by the Bush tax cuts.

In order to argue for tax increases, let's first look at what we have lost as a result of the Bush tax cuts. Assume for a moment the Bush tax cuts never took place. How much revenue would the top 1% have generated alone? If the Bush tax cuts were never enacted, the top 1% would have contributed 300 billion dollars more per year. One could say 300 billion isn't much compared to our overall budget and huge debt. However, 300 billion per year, over the past 10 years is three trillion dollars. Now add in the interest that we now owe on this three trillion dollars. With these tax cuts alone, our current debt could have been reduced by about a third. Our national debt is about three trillion dollars more than it needs to be, just by considering the Bush tax cuts for the wealthiest 1%.

The second biggest problem, which has affected our deficit and overall debt, is our decade-long and continued period of war. There has been debate over the actual costs of these wars. It is difficult to come up with an exact figure because there are so many aspects of the war that need to be accounted for, such as actual defense spending, veteran's benefits, extended medical costs, foreign aid, rebuilding assistance, homeland security, etc. From the beginning of the first action against Afghanistan, recent studies estimate the true cost to be anywhere from 3-4 trillion dollars.[xxxvi] Here again is another third or more of our current debt.

The most troubling part about these wars contributing

to our debt is that no one wants to pay for it! Throughout our history, from the beginning of our nation, we always paid for our wars in full. From the 1800s through WWI and WWII, to the later Korean and Vietnam conflicts, the government paid for these wars by selling government war bonds and raising taxes.[xxxvii] Even the first Bush, George Herbert W. Bush, after pledging to not raise taxes understood the need to raise taxes. Taxes needed to go up in order to pay for Operation Desert Storm, the first Iraq war. Throughout our history we have always raised taxes during times of war but decided not to do it for our wars in the past decade. Not only did we not raise taxes in a time of war, Bush Jr. cut taxes! How are we supposed to be serious about fiscal responsibility when pledges to not raise taxes prevent us from even paying for the things we need? Instead we've decided yet again to kick the can down the road for our children to pay.

These two areas alone, the Bush tax cuts and our unfunded wars, account for about 2/3s of our current debt. The other third of our debt can be attributed to a combination of other things. Entitlements, other sources of lost tax revenue, and two large bailout and stimulus packages all contributed to our debt as well. The necessity for the bailout package past by President Bush and the stimulus package passed a short time after by President Obama, in such crucial economic times is continually being contested.

Democrats Aren't Blameless Either

I like to consider myself a centrist on the political spectrum. I do admit and it may be no surprise that I lean more towards the left on many issues. I do however recognize that the far left is as much to blame for many of our problems.

First is their unyielding support of unions at any cost. In the previous section on unions we've outlined some of the reasons unions exist. But at the same time the Democratic defenders of unions have to stop defending all practices. Just because we may like unions, we still need to recognize the areas where high benefits, pensions, and excesses get out of control.

The other problem among radical Democrats is their belief that Social Security, Medicare and Medicaid are doing just fine, not causing a strain on our fiscal outlook. Extreme Democrats deny that there is anything to fix or adjust in these programs. In July of 2011, President Obama tried including changes to Social Security and Medicare as part of a debt negotiation deal. House Minority Leader, Nancy Pelosi stated that house Democrats oppose <u>any</u> changes to senior's entitlements.[xxxviii] I certainly am a champion to the benefits of these programs, but to deny that there isn't any problem supporting them at current levels is delusional. Especially as the baby-boomers are beginning to retire, we simply cannot afford to continue with business as usual. Certain cuts and adjustments will need to be made in order to sustain these programs. (Specifics on the problems facing Social Security and Medicare in Chapter 8) The longer we wait to fix these problems, the higher the probability that these programs will go belly up when the shit really does hit the fan. If we continue to stall reforms, we risk having to totally dissolve these programs when they really are in trouble.

Another point I would like to address concerning the failure of the left has been their defense of old, outdated, and some newly proposed regulations, that are unnecessary and can stifle innovation and growth.

One of the biggest burdens to businesses, especially small businesses can be taxes. As discussed earlier, corporate tax rates can be lowered for all businesses big and small, as long as loopholes are closed for the larger corporations. Another big obstacle to small business growth can be outrageous licensing requirements and the fees attached to them. Most business licenses and fees are imposed at the state and local levels of government. While most licensing is required in order to protect consumers, entrepreneurs in certain cities and towns can face grueling paperwork, a lengthy list of requirements, and heavily imposed fees. Democrats in state legislatures need to take a good look at their laws and make sure they are not over burdening small businesses with lengthy, unnecessary, and expensive licensing requirements.

Typically Republicans are against regulations and

Democrats support the need for regulating. I tend to agree with the Democrats when it comes to oversight, but we must acknowledge there are regulations that do need adjusting. Some regulations are flat out ridiculous; like ones that require African hair-braiders to get full cosmology licenses, which can require (depending on the state) up to $400 in fees, 400 days training, three exams, and a 12th grade minimum education.[xxxix]

This again is an area where we need to focus on balance. We can loose sight of the big picture when we focus on our single ideologies. Not all corporations are bad. Some are very proactive and progressive towards society. Not all regulations are good either. Of course we need to protect the people, but at what costs? Certain regulations aimed to protect the public may be a good idea on the surface. But the underlying costs and benefits need to be carefully weighed so they do not stifle ambitions, the economy and innovation, which can prevent people from achieving their American Dream.

Chapter 8
What We Need to Do

Our Country's Strength, a growing middle class

As mentioned earlier the strength of our country as a whole is dependent upon the strength and size of our middle class. The more people prosper the better our country is. This isn't just a moral objective but an economic objective. We need to understand that in order to sustain our country's growth we have to sustain the middle class.

I have already shown and few could argue that we have a serious problem with a shrinking middle class. The income gap is growing as the historical facts have shown us. Our previous chapters have given a good understanding as to what's been going on. Now let's connect the dots.

During WWI tax rates for the wealthiest individuals were 77%. In 1924, five years prior to the start of the Great Depression tax rates went from 77% for the highest earners to a historical low of 25%. This allowed for the greatest transfer of wealth back to the super wealthy, leading to the greatest income disparity between rich and poor that our country had ever seen. After the recent "Great Recession" in 2007, economists have been able to do comparative studies between these two times in our history. Most notable are the recent works of economist Emanuel Saez, professor at the University of California, Berkely and Thomas Picketty, from the Paris School of Economics. The results of their studies show an identical concentration of wealth in the hands of the wealthy during the periods leading up to the Great Depression and the recent recession in 2007. They believe that this income disparity is one of the key economic factors that helped lead us to these market crashes.[xl] The increasing wealth gap in the 1920s, characteristic of a weak middle class, could not sustain our economy and we saw what happened next, the Great Depression.

During the depression our politicians realized the need for a strong middle class and decided to help spur middle class growth by evening the playing field with tax rates on the wealthy above 70%. This new progressive tax system started in 1933 as part of Franklin Roosevelt's "New

Deal". By 1937 GDP and the unemployment rate returned to pre-depression levels. The New Deal, with its progressive tax system and large government spending initiatives remained mostly intact all the way up to the 1970s. During this time our country saw the biggest growth to the middle class and largest economic boom that the world has ever seen. There is still many of these "New Deal" programs functioning today, such as the SEC, the FHA, the FDIC, and Social Security.

Next came the late 1970s and 80s, a period where taxes were greatly reduced allowing for the lowest rates on the wealthy since before the Great Depression. Here we again start to see a growing gap between the rich and poor, a weakening middle class and this period was plagued with recessions and stagflation.

Then we move to the Clinton Era of the 90s. Understanding the need for progressive taxation Clinton raised the upper tax rates to 40%, and yet again we saw the largest jump to our economy in just over a decade. During the 90s, Median Household Income rose significantly for the first time in 20 years.

We all know what happened next; the Bush Era, where again our tax system digressed giving lower rates to the wealthy, especially in the form of significantly lowered capital gains rates. Once again we saw a huge growth in the disparity between rich and poor, which also means a struggling middle class. With this huge income gap we can guess based on past history what happened next. Our economy took a tailspin into the worst economic downturn since the Great Depression.

We have over 100 years experience now as an industrialized nation. We know that to have a strong economy we need a strong middle class. From our history of taxation we even have the proof as to what helps sustain a strong middle class. Proper progressive taxation isn't there to stifle innovation or punish those who do well. It is there to help sustain the middle class by keeping in check the tendencies of capitalism, that when left unchecked leads to a growing income gap between the rich and poor. A growing income gap means a sinking middle class, where a majority of people can no longer afford to support themselves. This leads to an unsustainable economy, which eventually transpires into recession or depression. And this isn't good for anyone. We have the history to prove this!

The Stalled Economy's biggest hurdle...Our Politicians

We have looked into the causes of the recent economic downturn. I hope to have convinced you that it was mostly due to the ever-increasing gap in wealth disparity and the destruction of the middle class. While the dust has settled from the recession and slow but steady gains have been made, we certainly have not fully dug ourselves out of this mess.

There is still high unemployment and a looming debt that is still growing. While these problems need to be addressed, relatively nothing of any significance has been done recently because of our politicians. The ones who are supposed to be fixing our problems can't do anything because of their politics.

You know we have a sad state of political affairs when people from the GOP, instead of working to fix problems have stated their main goal in office is to make the President lose any chance for reelection. The Republican Senate Minority Leader, Mitch McConnell has stated in numerous interviews that, "the single most important thing we want to achieve is for President Obama to be a one-term president."[xli] Paul Ryan and other Republican congressmen have echoed these sentiments as being the top Republican priority. From the start they put up obstacles in an attempt to prevent any positive outcomes from occurring under a Democratic president.

One example of political game playing in Congress involved the issue of raising our debt ceiling. The debt ceiling is a number that limits how much debt our Treasury is allowed to finance. The Treasury only handles our bills it doesn't create them. Congress creates the bills. Because our expenses have risen, the Treasury needs approval to finance this debt, mostly by selling bonds. Without the Treasury being allowed to finance and pay our bills, the United States of America would default on its obligations. Why is this important? It affects our credit rating, our trustworthiness as a nation, our interest rates would go up, and people who invest in America would pull out.

As inflation rises and as our GDP rises with our spending, this debt ceiling number needs to rise as well. This has been done 78 times since 1960. The debt ceiling was raised 18 times under President Reagan and seven times under George W. Bush.[xlii] So, why wouldn't Republicans in the House agree to raise the debt ceiling when the issue arose again in 2010? Republicans wanted to leverage our ability to pay the nation's bills as a call for big cuts in spending. They wished to risk defaulting, by not allowing the Treasury to pay for our obligations that Congress already approved, in exchange for Democrats agreeing to other issues.

It's no wonder the economy remains sluggish. Assume our country was like a big corporation. Think if you were an investor watching a session of Congress much like you'd watch a Board of Directors meeting. If that company's Board of Directors acted anything like the members of our Congress during this debt-ceiling charade, you wouldn't want to invest a single dime in that company. Hence our country's economy continues to be sluggish with the help of our Board of Directors who won't give first priority to the business of the country. Instead they'd rather play political games.

Where's the Job Creators?

Any time it is suggested to raise taxes on the wealthy or it is proposed to close tax loopholes for big corporations, we have heard the same excuse over and over as to why this is not a good idea. Many of you have heard the line "We shouldn't tax the job creators!" Since this excuse is used against any proposition to raise taxes on the wealthy or close loopholes for corporations, then the GOP must think and believe that it is the wealthy and big corporations who create the jobs. The GOP like to believe that keeping taxes low for these people gives them more cash, which enables them to hire more people. While it sounds like reasonable logic, the facts unfortunately give us a different story.

In March of 2012 the Federal Reserve estimated that American non-financial companies had 1.7 trillion dollars in domestic liquid assets.$_{xliii}$ A more recent study by David Cay Johnston, who looked at IRS figures from 2009, gives a much different figure. The numbers Johnston compiled from the IRS enabled him to see all cash reserves for American companies held worldwide. Johnston's total estimate for cash held by U.S. companies in 2009 was 5.1 trillion dollars. 5.1 trillion!$_{xliv}$

You may say to yourself, "So what if companies are holding some cash in reserve?" Well, "some" cash is one thing. 5.1 trillion dollars of cash is another story. Let's put five trillion dollars into perspective.

Let us assume it costs a business about $50,000 per worker hired, which covers an average salary, average benefits and the employer's portion of payroll taxes. With three trillion dollars, at $50K per worker, you can hire and pay for six million workers, for 10 years straight. How many workers is six million? Hiring six million new workers would bring our unemployment rate down to 4%. Or for the same three trillion dollars you could hire over the next 5 years a total of 12 million workers at $50,000 each and bring our unemployment rate down to 0%. Three trillion dollars is enough to bring unemployment down to 0% for five years. And three trillion dollars is also two trillion less than the five trillion estimated cash reserves held by U.S. companies.

Now remember from Chapter 6 that total federal tax revenue in recent years has only been about 2.2 trillion dollars, which leads us to ask another question. If we are to believe the answer to job growth is lower taxes for corporations and the wealthy, how much of the collected 2.2 trillion in federal revenue do corporations need returned, adding to their already five trillion dollar cash reserves, before they will begin to add jobs back to the economy? In 2011 corporations paid 181 billion dollars total in corporate taxes.$_{xlv}$ Even if the federal government gave back all income tax paid by corporations, this would only be a small amount compared to the five trillion dollars these companies already hold in liquid assets. How much more money does a company need before they will start creating jobs? The answer is; they don't need more money from tax breaks. There are other reasons why companies are not creating jobs. It's not because of too much tax like the GOP would lead you to believe.

If slow job growth isn't due to a shortage of cash, then why is there still little job growth? Instead there are two other key ingredients required for economic growth. First is confidence in the market. With a weak economy and a middle class with little disposable income, big companies are skeptical to expand production, hiring additional workers. Big companies that are doing ok at the moment have already maximized their profits according to today's market. If they have already been able to maximize profits at current levels, why should they risk new investments? Simon Tilford, chief economist at the Center for European Reform also believes the reason corporations aren't growing is because of executive pay structures. Tilford says, "distorted incentives for senior executives, who's pay is based on short-term performance rather than long term investments" is one key factor behind the lack of job creation from big companies.[xlvi]

The second and probably bigger issue is the lack of ideas and innovations from those who actually have capital and resources. With a huge income disparity and a large portion of the five trillion dollars in corporate cash holdings, left in the hands of a few large companies, the "idea pool" (much like that of a gene pool) is severely limited. While we are relying on the few who have wealth to create and innovate, there is a whole slew of other people and small businesses that have ideas, but no capital or resources needed to grow those ideas into businesses and jobs.

Small businesses and new start-ups represent 99.7% of all employers. Over the past 17 years, small businesses accounted for 65% of all newly created jobs. When it comes to ideas and innovations, small businesses and start-ups produce 13 times more patents per employee than do large firms and corporations.[xlvii]

So it is obvious that if we want to create jobs, then we have to make investment capital available to all those who do have the ideas and will to innovate. Big businesses already have access to large reserves of cash. Even if a large company doesn't have huge cash reserves on hand, they still have credit, which gives them access to capital loans if they want to grow. However there are millions of other people with ideas that don't have the prospects to turn their ideas into businesses. In the past, people from the middle class trying to start a business have been able to use their own savings, mortgage their homes, or get loans with good credit. But in the recent economic environment with a struggling middle class, these new innovators don't have the same prospects and access to capital that they used to have. Economist and Nobel laureate, Peter Diamond says we need to put money and access to capital back in the hands of the middle class. He suggests doing this with a progressive tax code that helps to grow the middle class. Diamond eloquently describes our problem of slow job growth by saying we shouldn't focus on tax breaks for "those who have already created jobs, but focus on those who 'would-be' job creators".[xlviii]

Education, Education, Education!

Another big problem facing our country and our economic future is our decline in education at all levels. This is an issue that should concern all of us, those with and without children. It is not just a problem for our children but our whole economy, country and future.

The facts are that America's grades at all levels, when compared to those of other countries have been slipping significantly. Out of the OECD countries (Organization for Economic Cooperation and Development), the United States ranked 17th in reading and didn't even make the top 20 in both Math and Science.[xlix] Why is this a big problem? Because in today's global economy American workers and workers from around the globe are all competing for the same jobs.

It seems everyday I'm reading in the newspaper about budget cuts in education. Schools are cutting teachers, slashing extracurricular activities and getting rid of art, music and other extracurricular classes. The state of Colorado cut 260 million dollars for education in 2010. Cuts in Michigan totaled 382 million and Virginia cut 700 million dollars for K-12 funding. Because of education cuts in Florida, tuition in the state's public colleges and universities increased 32% from 2009-2011. 9,400 students lost financial aid grants due to cuts in Minnesota. Arizona eliminated preschools for 4,328 children. Over the past three years 34 states cut budgets for K-12 education and 43 states cut funding to public colleges and universities.₁ How is our country supposed to succeed in this global market when we keep cutting funds to one of the most important factors that will help our economy and future? Especially if we want to continue to be a country of innovation and compete in today's high tech world we need to educate more, not less.

There are reports that even in today's economy with such high unemployment, there are companies hiring in the U.S. with job openings waiting to be filled. But a common problem has been that there is no one with the skills and education needed to fill them. A recent study by the Manufacturing Institute estimates in early 2012 there were 600,000 job openings in U.S. manufacturing that were unable to be filled. The CEOs of Siemens, GE and Boeing have all spoken openly about a lack of educated and skilled workers needed to fill current job openings in their companies.ₗᵢ What does this tell you?

Here is another example of where greater tax revenue from corporations and the wealthy are directly beneficial to businesses. Better funding for our children's education directly affects businesses here in America. Increased tax revenue for better education gives businesses the skilled and qualified people needed to run and handle their businesses.

Of course it's not enough to just fund, fund, fund. We need teachers too, good teachers. Rewarding teachers with better pay and bonuses for student achievement can give an incentive for teachers to do better and attracts better educators. The whole system needs a long overdue restructuring.

We need a system that does all the above. We need to attract and reward talented teachers and stop protecting the ones that aren't doing their job. We can accomplish this by finding better ways to evaluate teacher performance fairly and comprehensively by examining the teachers and the students they teach. We can do this.

But no improvements can be made if we are just slashing budgets, asking teachers to do more with less. Instead of slashing budgets this is one investment we should be doubling down on.

Those who oppose education being public would rather defund it, without providing current feasible alternatives. Extreme conservatives would like to see education handled by the private sector. But remember, when a large number of people can't afford private education, many kids will be denied the equal opportunity to receive an education. Cutting education budgets puts our children, our economy and the entire future of our country at risk.

Fiscal Conservatives? Then pay our debts!

America does have a serious current and future fiscal problem. Simply put, we've spent a lot more than we have taken in from tax revenue. I believe, as I'm sure many Americans do, that we need to get our financial house in order and we need to pay off our debt. We have now incurred a total debt reaching 14 trillion dollars. Such a huge debt is probably the single biggest hindrance to our country's economy now. Our credit rating has been downgraded and because of it, businesses are skeptical to invest in the United States.

So how do we bring our debt under control? Quite simply, we pay for it! And how do we pay for it? With taxes! In order to get our <u>future</u> yearly deficits under control we need to cut spending in the things we don't need and that are wasteful. But we still have to pay for the things we do want and need. The question <u>now</u> is who's going to pay for the things we've already bought? Our children or us? The Republicans argue to not pay for our debt by raising any taxes. Instead they propose to just cut spending. Republicans want the money saved from spending cuts to eventually pay down our debt. There are two problems with this thinking. The first is that with current tax revenues, government spending would have to be cut drastically. In 2011 our yearly federal deficit was about 1.5 trillion dollars. In order to balance the budget by just cuts alone, we would need to cut 40 percent, almost half of all government spending.[lii] If we were to cut 40% of our entire government, we risk our country falling apart by not investing in the things we need.

The second problem with the Republican plan is that

it allows today's generation to have gotten away scot-free by over spending, buying things on credit and not paying for them. To put it in the simplest terms, let's say you purchase cable TV service for your home and don't pay the cable bill for a whole year, racking up a past due bill of $1,000. What the Republicans propose to do is not pay for the $1,000 in services we received. Instead they want to cut the cable service so we don't have any future bills. Republicans want to take the money our kids could have used to buy cable in the future and instead use it to pay off our debts for the cable services we bought. Is this a responsible solution for our children? Republicans can talk all they want about cutting future spending but the fact is we still have a huge bill that we need to pay for now, not our children. Even if we did only cut future spending we would still be pushing off our past credit bills onto our children.

We constantly hear our politicians using the phrase "kick the can down the road". Republicans have used this phrase as an argument to cut future spending. They say that if we continue to rack up deficits it will fall on our kids to pay. I agree that if we don't make cuts we will continue to add to our debt. But even the Republican idea to only cut future spending is still kicking the can down the road. It means that future generations will still have to pay for our past debts, not by paying more taxes but by receiving fewer services in the future. The only way to not "kick the can down the road" is to get the people of today to pay for the debts we have accrued. Anything short of raising taxes today or even retroactively raising taxes over past years, would still be a form of "kicking the can down the road".

If those who call themselves fiscal conservatives are truly concerned about fiscal responsibility, they should realize the only true fiscally responsible thing to do, would be for this generation to pay for the things we bought. And how do we pay for these things? With taxes!

Social Security and Medicare, as it relates to Current and Future Deficits

One point used by the GOP as an answer to fixing our

fiscal disorder is our spending on entitlements such as Social Security and Medicare. While these programs do have problems that need to be fixed, they cannot be used as items when discussing our current debt and here's why.

First off, Social Security and Medicare are paid for with separate payroll taxes not federal income taxes. Not only have separate payroll taxes been used to fully pay for all Social Security and Medicare spending, there is even a surplus of 3.5 trillion dollars. These programs have taken in 3.5 trillion dollars more over the years then it has spent. What happens is these payroll taxes go into the Social Security Trust Fund? The excess money not spent has been given back to the government in the form of bonds, to help pay for other government expenses. Over the years the government has used our payroll taxes intended for Social Security and Medicare on other things.   Don't worry, the government is supposed to pay back these bonds.

This shows that past and current fiscal problems are not due to Social Security and Medicare. Many politicians, especially the GOP want to use these programs as a source to cut spending when Social Security and Medicare programs have never incurred one penny of debt and the excess funds from these programs have gone on to help finance other government outlays. Yes, Social Security and Medicare do face their own problems in the near future, which will need to be reformed and addressed, but none of our current deficit and debt is due to these programs. Social Security and Medicaid have paid for themselves in full and under current rules can still support themselves until 2033 and 2024 respectively.[liii]

The fact that these programs can only support themselves in their current form for only another few years does mean that we will have to make changes to these programs. However, our current debt is not a result of Social Security and Medicare spending, but is due to the other things we've bought. So, take Social Security, Medicare and payroll taxes out of the equation and we still have a massive debt to pay.

When Republicans suggest using cuts in Social Security and Medicare to help pay the debt, they are suggesting that we lower these expenses in order to use future surpluses from Social Security and Medicare to pay down the debt. Cuts in Social Security and Medicare will likely need to happen for their own future sustainability. However, proposed massive cuts to these programs in order to use payroll taxes to help finance other government expenditures, represents a drastic unfair tax ploy on average Americans and a big "get out of jail free card for the wealthy", and here is why...

As explained in Chapter 6, those who make under $106,000 pay 5.65% (9.1% for self-employed) in Social Security and Medicare taxes. Those who earn above $106,000 pay a substantially lower rate in payroll taxes as they earn more.   For example someone who is self-employed and makes $600,000 a year only pays 9.1% on the first $106,000, which would be only 1.6% of their overall income. Now let us assume Social Security and Medicare benefits are cut and payroll taxes remain the same so that there is a continued surplus in the Social Security and Medicare Funds. After enacting these cuts, let's assume the fund amasses a 1 trillion dollar surplus and it is this surplus that goes to help fund our debt for other government expenditures like defense spending. What you now have is 1 trillion dollars being used to help fund other areas of government. The average Americans contributed 5.65% of their income towards this fund and someone who makes $600,000 per year only contributed 1.6%. So much for a progressive tax system, this would be a completely digressive use of the tax system.

This is why arguments used to support cuts in Social Security and Medicare for the sole purpose of paying down our debt incurred by other spending would be a travesty to the average American and a double win-win for those who earn more. Our debt, in order to be fair should be paid for by a fair and progressive tax increase on us today not cuts for tomorrow's seniors.

Facing the Facts on Social Security and Medicare

While I have just opposed Social Security and Medicare cuts as a path for today's debt reduction, we still cannot deny that the future of Social Security and Medicare themselves are in trouble. These programs have done remarkably well. They have funded themselves and served its intended function of providing a safety net for those in retirement over the past 70 years. At current levels it is estimated that they can still sustain themselves until 2033 for Social Security and 2024 for Medicaid. These deadlines are quick to come upon us, and something needs to be done before these programs start contributing to our debt as well.

There are a few factors threatening the continued path of these programs. The first and biggest problem is not the fault of any politician or party; it is demographics. Due to our country's age demographic, more people will be retiring and taking out from the system then younger people can put back in. This has already happened. For the first time in history, over the past five years, Social Security and Medicare have begun to pay out more money than they are taking in. Please note that these programs aren't in debt yet. They still have the 3.5 trillion owed to them from the surpluses they have saved over the years. Each year's deficit will be filled by this surplus until the funds run out or unless we do something about it.

These are the facts and Democrats need to wake up and smell what is just around the corner. The sooner we do something about it the better. The longer we wait, the worse the problem becomes and the likelihood of saving these programs fades.

What are the factors we need to look at when seeking ways to solve this problem? The main problem as I just mentioned is demographics. With the baby boomers starting to enter retirement there simply are not enough young workers to support all future outlays. The other factor in our country's demographics is that people are now living longer. Average life expectancy has risen from age 69 in 1960 to age 79 in 2009. Since retirees are living 10 years longer on average than was expected 50 years ago, the system is paying out more than expected.

Another serious problem to Medicare's expenses is the skyrocketing cost of healthcare. Add on to that the recent addition of Medicare Part B, which pays for senior's prescription drugs, and we have a system where payroll taxes from younger workers will not be able to cover all these costs.

The first real attempt to tackle rising medical costs was done so in part with the new healthcare law, which so many have deemed "Obamacare". While this bill has added government spending in some areas and new requirements placed on insurance companies, the main focus of the healthcare law was an attempt to lower rising medical costs. Congress did this in the interest of not just cheaper healthcare for all, but more importantly to try and lower the foreseen rising expenditures for Medicare and Medicaid. The full healthcare law doesn't take effect until 2014 and it will probably be another two years after which, before we can see if the law has any positive effects on healthcare costs. As necessary as it is to try and control medical costs, it is only a part of what needs to be accomplished.

Just as Republicans need to wake up and understand the need for more revenue through taxes in order to pay our debt, Democrats need to wake up and understand that real reforms to Social Security and Medicare are needed. I believe we can reform these systems while still preserving the original purpose behind these programs.

These programs were originally intended to be a safety net, not a full fledged retirement plan that would allow you to live your retirement free of all responsibilities. People were still supposed to plan and save for retirement. These programs were intended to be a minimum safety net so that even if something bad happened, such as a stock market crash where you lost most of your savings, you would still have something to fall back on.

With this in mind a combination of steps need to be taken so that Social Security can be sustained without delivering a hard blow to seniors. The longer we wait on choosing to enact reforms the harder the reforms will need to be in future years.

The first possible reform is that the retirement age should be raised slightly, especially since we are living a lot longer. This can be done on a fair gradual scale. Right now people can retire and receive benefits as early as 62 years old with full benefits at age 67. A gradual two-year increase would help substantially. Another helpful reform would be eliminating payments to some people based on those who have substantial non-Social Security income. The person who earned $600,000 a year and was able to amass investments in the millions of dollars, who paid 1.6% of their income into Social Security has done really well. They are lucky enough to not need these safety net payouts. Think of Social Security and Medicare as an insurance plan. You pay into it and hopefully you do well enough that you don't ever need it.

Another main component that needs to be addressed is the role of people's personal responsibility when it comes to planning for retirement. Yes, the safety net of Social Security and Medicare are needed and should be preserved. We can preserve it for the purpose of a safety net. But Social Security never was intended to be a full retirement program that allowed for people to retire free and clear of any worry. Too many have neglected the responsibility of saving themselves. Social Security was set up as a guarantee in the event you lost your savings in a market crash, it wasn't intended to be a replacement for people having to take responsibility and save on their own. As discussed earlier the government can help people save substantially more by raising contribution limits to tax deferred savings accounts.

The bottom line is we can't continue to pay out more than we take in for much longer. Democrats need to wake up to the idea that something must be done if we are to preserve the original purpose of Social Security and Medicare as a safety net.

Separation of Merch and State

Our democracy is based on a government by the people and for the people. How is our government controlled by the people?...with votes! We have the choice to vote for those who we believe would best represent our ideals and beliefs. We elect people to lead us through our issues and problems by enacting laws and policies in the hope that we may all prosper.

Our votes for or against certain issues, policies and the leaders we choose to enact them, are only as good as the information we are given to make good informed decisions.

Most of us heard the term "information is power", and

it is! This is why dictators and aristocracies around the world control and limit all media in their country. China, Syria, Saudi Arabia, North Korea and a number of other countries have only strict state-controlled TV stations, newspapers and other media outlets. They do this in order to control information given to the public, so they may remain in power by eliminating any opposing views that would threaten their leadership and power. Most of these countries even have strict filters and blocks on the Internet, all in an effort to control information.

We in the United States however have a free press. It is believed that one requirement for a functioning democracy is where the public could be informed with information and opinions free of government censorship or control. This is why many have referred to the press as an unofficial fourth branch of government. This fourth branch keeps a check over the other three branches of government by giving people factual, uncensored information, empowering the people to make informed voting decisions concerning their government.

But over the years our information has started to become controlled; not by the government but by money. The money behind corporate America has funded most of the information our politicians and us receive from the media. Information given to us, filtered through biased corporate conglomerates cannot be trusted to serve the interests of the people. Corporate money is spent to sway people minds, views, and votes, to serve the interests of those providing the financial support to our media outlets.

Many proponents in favor of using money to influence policies and votes would say it is a free country to do so. We do live in a free country. However, the paradox arises where we are supposed to have a system of "one man=one vote". In our society we are all equal and each vote gets an equal say. We are all able to share our thoughts and opinions, but should one person, simply because they are wealthy be allowed to influence information and policy? Allowing someone to spend millions of dollars to support a candidate or issue gives one man a disproportionate influence of one person's view compared to others.

This special interest money has been making its way into our system in three key areas: In the form of lobbying, media control, and campaign finance. Of course lobbying has been going on since we can all remember. Money gives access and influence over our elected officials to sway policies in favor of the people with money. There has been much outrage and distaste for the effects lobbying has had on our political system. Apparently there hasn't been enough vocal outrage considering nothing has been done to curtail the influence of special interests in Washington.

Then there is the money behind corporate media. A few corporations (about six media giants) have bought up and own 90% of our TV, print, and radio media.[liv] Six mega-companies control 90% of the information we receive and are able to tailor this information to suit their own interests.

Aside from typical mass media, the growing influence of the Internet has proven to be a blessing and a curse. The Internet has enabled millions of people to become their own media outlets. From bloggers to independent publishing, the Internet has given millions of people a voice they never had. While the information age is a great phenomenon brought about by the Internet, it also has its drawbacks. Information has become abundant and easily accessible, but there is almost too much of it that is unreliable, biased or just plain untrue. It is getting harder and harder for a person surfing the web to trust and organize all the information that is out there, especially when anyone with a computer can type and post whatever they want. But even on the Internet, corporate media still rules. With huge cash reserves, large media conglomerates purchase search engines allowing them to place content that sways search engines to sites of their choosing.

Then finally there is the issue of campaign finance; money raised by candidates running for office. The issue here is that candidates running for office can curtail their policy decisions to favor the largest donors.

What can we do about all of this? First, we can demand free and fair elections by supporting campaign finance reforms that limits private money from influencing campaigns. But the most important thing we can all do as responsible citizens is to be weary of what we see, hear and read. We should take the effort to do some of our own research. When you hear a statement or figure, don't simply accept it for the truth. Ask some of your own questions and look around for the answers. As we mentioned earlier, the Internet is a blessing and a curse. While it is full of misinformation, it is a good tool that can be utilized and still has a lot of good information. Again, ask the questions: Who, what, where, why and how. When looking to solve a crime, detectives often say, "Follow the money" and it will lead us to the perpetrator. The same could be said when scrutinizing the information we are given. Try to pay attention to who is giving you the information. Who signs their paycheck and what financial interests that company or person may have. Pay attention to what you read or hear and ask yourself where and who you heard it from and where did they get their information. But most importantly don't let politicians and pundits play on your fears. Be weary when you hear people use generalized statements to support a more complicated issue. Do the research and ask the questions. We've relied for too long on the evening news and television to give us our information, which is no longer dependable. Be weary of bias and don't simply accept what you hear.

Obama's Policies (Failed?)

For the first time in history we have seen a truly global economic recession. In this modern world of globalization, what happens in one country or region now more than ever significantly affects other countries and regions. While the United States has had its recession, so has Europe and Asia experienced their own economic slow downs. Even though the U.S. is still facing hard times and unemployment above 8%, we are faring much better than our European counterparts. The only countries that grew faster at the beginning of 2012 were China, India, Japan, Australia and Canada. These are all countries that the extreme right would complain have too many socialist government policies.[iv] While Europe is normally considered more socialistic, they for the first time in decades have tried to enact drastic cuts and austerity measures, which has kept their growth rates far below the rest of the world. At the time I'm writing this, most economists are starting to agree that recent cuts and austerity imposed on Greece, Spain and others, have driven these countries into deeper recessions.[lvi] President Obama can take some credit. The large stimulus package, passed in 2009, worked in comparison to the policies of those countries in Europe that have fared much worse than us. It kept people employed and helped to keep afloat industries such as automobile and construction businesses.

Of course doing better than Europe is no cause for celebration when we still have problems. But what else can the government do to help, especially since Republicans are saying Obama's policies have failed? The other single biggest policy that the government controls which has a major effect on the economy is our budget and tax policy. We have been operating under the same Bush tax rates over the past 10 years. Although Obama and Democrats have tried to change this, Republicans in Congress have not allowed for any tax increases. So how can anyone say that Obama's policies have failed when a Republican controlled House of Representatives won't allow any of his major economic policies, such as tax increases to be enacted?

If Obama has failed anywhere, it would be that he hasn't been able to convince Republican members of Congress that tax increases are needed. He has convinced most of the American people, as about 70% of Americans approved of the Buffet tax increase.[lvii] But the Republican constituents in the House turned down this measure ignoring the will of the American people.

Even though the revenues that the Buffet Tax would have raised were small in comparison to the overall national debt, think how much more it would look as a percentage of our national debt if it were enacted 10 years ago. If these funds were being put towards our deficit this whole time, it would add up to a lot more and quick. Remember as I have shown earlier, the Bush tax cuts alone for the top 1% have contributed to about 1/3 of our current debt over the past 10 years. The Buffet tax was just one measure that was put forth to Congress and failed to pass.

So, how can Obama's policies have failed when none of his major economic reforms, such as those relating to taxes have been allowed to pass due to Republican obstructionism?

Chapter 9

Our Government At Work

Our Tax Dollars at Work. The Things we did together.

NASA: Our space exploration program. As I am writing this, CNN is showing the space shuttle Discovery being retired to the Smithsonian museum. This is the last of the space shuttles being grounded forever. NASA and its space program has been one of the great American achievements that was only made possible due to a collective initiative by our country and our collective tax dollars. But NASA didn't only fly big machines into space.

Over the years, research and development that went into the space program spawned many other innovations that most of us don't readily know about. NASA has thousands of technological patents that are used extensively by today's private companies. Things such as Teflon, pacemakers, satellite technology, and infrared technology used in home thermometers, were all byproducts of NASA's R&D. The space program also developed water filter technology, cordless tools, memory foam and a long list of other innovations.   NASA is just one example where the collective force of America has achieved greatness.   You may believe that space exploration is a waste of tax dollars but what you shouldn't forget is all the other technologies and innovations that spawned as a result of NASA's research.

Please take a look at NASA's spinoff website which lists most of the products used today that utilizes technology developed by NASA.[lviii]

NASA is just one grand example where collective research and development has helped develop the world we live in today. The Department of Defense, while serving its main role protecting America, has a long list of technologies from its own research and development that impact our lives today and are used in many private sector enterprises. The jet engine, GPS technology, nuclear technology, and common things like synthetic rubber, were all developed by our tax dollars. While the exact beginning of the computer is debated, there should be no doubt that the Department of Defense was a large contributor, leading innovations in the fields of computer and internet technology, whose impact on today's world can not be ignored or denied.

We could fill an entire book with other grand projects financed by the U.S. government. Initiatives and projects that have had huge impacts on our society and the world today, such as the Hoover Dam and the Tennessee Valley Authority (TVA), were both government projects that helped bring electricity and jobs to millions at the beginning of the 20th century.

Transport systems like the Erie Canal, which enabled access from the Northeast Atlantic to the Midwest Great Lakes was another grand government project. Let's not forget that the Panama Canal, which greatly benefits and helps businesses efficiently ship goods around the world was also paid for with our tax dollars. Then the advent of our train system, while largely led by private companies was made possible by government funded bonds and land grants.

The point here is not to say that the U.S. government is the ultimate end all to innovation. Nor is my intention to diminish the innovations and progress led by private companies, which our free market system helped grow. The main goal here is to remind us and show that our superior economic history is based on both private and government enterprises. It is because of the two working together that we have been able to achieve so much.

Another thing to remember is that projects such as the Hoover Dam and the development of satellite technology were too big for any one company to undertake. These grand projects were only possible at the time due to our collective will and yes, our collective tax dollars. Without the tax dollars none of this would have been possible.

The Military aren't the Only Ones Who Protect Us.

Throughout our recent history the budget for our military has been the single biggest outlay of all federally financed programs. The buildup of our military and its budget has served to protect our homeland and our families. The Cold War with the former U.S.S.R. served as a catalyst for this extreme military build-up, starting at the end of WWII. In 2009 we spent about 660 Billion dollars on national defense, which was about 19% of all federal spending. For the past 40 years our spending on defense has been between 15-25% of our overall budget.[lix] It is obvious that we have been willing to spend enormous sums of money in the name of "National Defense" and "National Security." However, the military aren't the only ones who protect our security. Bullets and bombs from a foreign nation aren't the only things that can kill you and your family.

While the military protects us from foreign threats, we have the FDA, the FAA, the CDC, the EPA, and FEMA, all of which are federally funded programs designed to protect our safety and security. This is just a short list of government organizations designed to protect us; there are many others as well. Today, we hear strong rhetoric by Republicans who claim the only thing these organizations do is hamper business growth, unnecessary, and hence should be cut. While each of these programs may have some of their own shortcomings, they were each set up to oversee and tackle real problems that occurred in the past. This means there were other real threats that our government saw a need to protect against.

The Food and Drug Administration protects us by making sure our food and medicines do not cause us harm. Its history begins in 1906 with Theodore Roosevelt and was later expanded by Franklin Roosevelt in 1938. Theses new initiatives were a direct response to hundreds of instances where death and sickness were being caused by toxic and adulterated products sold to the public.

The CDC or Center For Disease Control was founded in 1942. Its main function at the time was to battle Malaria, which was epidemic in the Southeastern United States. Throughout the years, the CDC has been charged with tackling other life threatening diseases, developing vaccination policies, and protecting us against other dangers to public health.

The Environmental Protection Agency isn't just a result of some tree huggers who warn against climate change and saving the whales. It was actually first proposed and formed by Republican President Richard Nixon in 1970. The EPA wasn't designed to be an obstacle to business. It is there to protect you and me! The EPA is responsible for testing and regulating our nation's water supplies, making sure all our water is safe to drink. They monitor air quality and try to limit toxins that private industries release into the air. The EPA also oversees waste removal including radioactive waste and pesticide controls, all of which are abundant and damaging to human health. While the EPA may have its own bureaucratic problems, its mission and purpose is clear. We should look to help improve their ability to protect the people and our environment while causing the least disruption to business, but not by compromising the health and safety of our citizens.

These programs I've listed are just a few of the organizations paid for with tax dollars that are charged with protecting our health and security. The funding for all these programs combined, still doesn't amount to the budget of our military. Do we need to go back to the times before these programs were developed, allowing thousands more to die again before we can recognize the important functions these programs provide to our society? Or can we just remember our history and why we have formed these departments originally? If we have so much concern for our safety that we spend 15-25% of our budget on the military, wouldn't we also want to further fund these programs that saves and protects lives as well.

Let's also not forget the good work our police and fire departments do. The functions of these departments and the jobs they create, which are funded by tax dollars serve us all everyday. Unfortunately over the past few years, with a slow economy, our police and fire department budgets have been hurt the most from both state and federal levels of funding.[ix]

Deficiencies in Efficiency

One final point to address is the argument or belief made by those on the right who say "private enterprise does it better" or that private industry can provide services more efficiently. This belief is one of the arguments used by the Republican Party to support the idea of turning government functions over to private industry to handle. My question is; who says private industry is more efficient? Where's the proof?

Turning over government services to private companies has already been attempted many times with some positive outcomes and some failures. The privatized prisons in Pennsylvania that we addressed in Chapter 5, showed systematic corruption where the company paid off judges to issue more and stricter sentences. Private companies who were given the task of providing military housing failed when they were not able to meet basic health and safety standards. Neglect by a private company at a Virginia military housing development was shown to have caused widespread mold problems that made many military families sick.[lxi]

Then there is the issue of wasteful spending. Many will say that government, because of its bureaucracy makes government highly inefficient. However large corporations also have their own bureaucratic webs to deal with. How many of you work for private companies where you still need to go through a long list of approvals before you can get something done? I'm sure many of you have experienced something like this. And government is no different.

The other assumption made is that private businesses don't waste money, which is highly untrue. Especially if a private company is providing a service paid for with tax dollars, some of that money is going directly into the company's profit margins not the services we require, which could be considered a waste of the people's tax dollars. Secondly, who's to say private industry doesn't waste money? I've been working in the private sector all my life and have always seen private companies wasting money. With large CEO pay packages, expensive office furniture and corporate jets, who can say private business doesn't waste money? Let's not forget the highly risky investments recently undertaken by the private banks. Wasn't this a big waste of investor's money, which then required the U.S. taxpayer to bail them out?

There is another argument to be made in the matter of who can do a better job providing the public services we need. Private business in the free market can do very well, but the opposite is also true. Private Businesses can fail and go bankrupt! If charging private business to handle things like educating our children or running public transportation, can we afford for that company to go bankrupt and shut down?   What about our water and sanitation facilities? Imagine what would happen if we had a purely free market system where our water and sewage was operated by a private company without any controls. Can a town afford to have its privately owned water and sewage suppliers go under? And if a private company that supplies services required by the public goes under, it still falls on the government to sort it out or bail them out. That's the thing about services provided by the government in the name of the common good. It can't fail! That is as long as we the voters decide to not let it fail.

One final point here needs to be made. While profit motive, which drives private companies to produce in the most efficient and cheapest ways may sound attractive, there is also a negative side. Being efficient and cheap in the short run can lead to further spending in the long run. Companies don't manufacture products to last a long time. They want to make a good product, but they also want you to keep coming back to buy more. Can we as a nation afford to buy a product or service from a private company just so we have to continue to pay that company to fix, refurbish and upgrade constantly. Let's say the government passes the job of bridge construction solely to a private firm. Are they going to build the best bridge with the best materials, put together in the strongest way possible so that the bridge will last us at least 50 years? Or will they try to build the bridge with the cheapest materials, using building methods that cost the least, which could mean the bridge only lasts 10 years before it needs to be fixed and refurbished. Is this a more efficient way for our government to operate and use our tax dollars?

We have already discussed in previous chapters the issues where pure capitalism and pure profit motive fails to support the good of the country. We have also looked at certain circumstances when the laws of supply and demand fail to create balanced markets. I don't mean to belittle the undeniably great things that capitalism has brought to our country and society. There are thousands of private companies that have done great things. But we also need to remember the great things that we as a people have accomplished as well, through our government and public funding. Many publicly funded accomplishments would have been highly improbable if they were handled solely by private business. It is only when capitalism, balanced with our long history of socialistic practices work together that we can have a truly balanced and efficient market.

Speaking From Personal Experience

It was 2004 when I made my first visit to Kuala Lumpur, Malaysia while traveling on tour. It was on this trip that I met my future ex-wife. I soon returned to visit her again, followed by a trip she took to visit me in the U.S. Finally, I decided to go for it and moved to Kuala Lumpur, trying to see if we could make a relationship work. This was 2005 when I took a year off from the music and touring business.

During this time I was not allowed to work in Malaysia as I only had a visitor visa. However, because of my entrepreneurial spirit I was working extensively trying to find other possible business opportunities in Malaysia that I could possibly pursue.

Moving to Kuala Lumpur (the capital city of Malaysia, which many simply refer to as KL) was a bit of a culture shock, but there were many parts of the country that I loved. I loved the food as well as certain parts of the culture and most people I met were very friendly. But there were days when I was completely frustrated and fed up with certain aspects of living in Kuala Lumpur.

The first thing about Malaysia that I didn't care for was the high heat and humidity, which was enough to wear anyone down. Then another major point of frustration was the horrible road system and immense traffic. Traffic in KL made driving in Los Angeles feel like a summer picnic. In KL, what should be an easy ten-minute drive with no traffic would easily turn into me being stuck in traffic for an hour and a half, at anytime without any notice. Then assuming you got to where you were going, the next task was finding a place to park. Overcrowded streets and small parking garages left me searching at times for over an hour. Adding to the traffic on the smaller side streets were the hundreds of cars illegally double-parked, blocking lanes that were supposed to be used for active driving. People would park anywhere they could, as there was little police enforcement of parking

Then there was the unreliability of our utilities. The electricity and water would get cut constantly without any seemingly good reason, almost on a weekly basis. Our phone and Internet connections would also cease to work at random times quite frequently. Even when the Internet was working, most of the time it was extremely slow.

Then I had my frustrations while trying to conduct business. When speaking to local friends and colleagues about my aspirations for starting a business, they would warn me "don't get discouraged, but things operate pretty slow around here." I would soon find out what they were talking about. People were chronically late to business meetings and appointments. When they finally arrived, people would say, "Sorry, la! Bad jam!" referring to the bad traffic. And I'm not talking about 10 minutes late. People would typically be late by an hour or more. Than there were problems trying to find and distribute information. There were few good phone books or places to reference local business information.

When conducting business in the U.S. it is typical to say, "I'll send it to you in the mail. You'll have it in a few days." However in Malaysia the mail system was slow and unreliable. Then if you had digital files to share, using the slow and unreliable Internet connections would make having to upload and download files difficult to impossible sometimes, especially if you were dealing with large files. Because of the slow mail and Internet, people would choose to just "meet up, and I'll pass it to you." But trying to meet someone on the other side of town could mean another three hours out of your day due to the horrible layout of the roads and traffic.

Than one day it dawned on me; aside from the heat, most of my frustrations with daily life and the difficulties while trying to conduct business, all had a common theme. All these difficulties were due to a lack of infrastructure. All these aspects of daily life were not as much a problem in the U.S. because we have the infrastructure to easily handle these things. Infrastructure set up by the government and funded with tax dollars makes life and business in the U.S. that much easier. In America we have some of the best roads and highways in the world. Our public utilities such as water and electricity operate very efficiently. Aside from severe storms and planned maintenance you could count on these utilities working. While the phone and Internet providers in the U.S. are private companies, much of the groundwork for these systems has been funded with the help of the American government and the American taxpayer. Then there is the U.S. Postal Service, where a letter mailed locally could be received as soon as the next day and a letter mailed from New York could reach California in as fast as three days. Being accustomed to having these functioning public systems in the U.S, is why I was so frustrated trying to live and work in Malaysia without them.

Next for me came 2007 into 2008 when my marriage started to fall apart. As the discussion of divorce came up, my first concern was for my son who was two years old at the time. Would he be able to come back to the U.S. with me or would his mother keep him in Malaysia? Of course I wanted my son to live with me back in America, not just for my own selfish reasons but because I believed he could have a better upbringing in the U.S. Of course this led to many fights with his mother who wanted our son to stay with her in Malaysia. While trying to form an argument as to why it would be better for him to grow up in the U.S. I proceeded to make a list of pros and cons between our two countries.

At the top of my list was education. Undeniably the public education system in the U.S. is far better than that in Malaysia. Then on my list I had a bunch of other things pertaining to the simpler aspects of growing up as a child. Certain things you may not think about and take for granted like sidewalks. None of the neighborhoods in Malaysia have sidewalks! Not all neighborhoods in the U.S. have them either but many do. Sidewalks are great for kids to be able to safely walk, ride a bike or roller-skate around the neighborhood, without having to go into the street. Next on my list were parks. There are so many great parks in the U.S. for kids to play. Most parks in the U.S. have jungle gyms, some have ponds and most every town has baseball and soccer fields. The park where I live now in Tennessee has tennis courts, volleyball courts, bike paths, a lake and other wide open spaces all nicely maintained, unlike the ones in Malaysia. Another thing on my list that was better in the U.S. were our cleaner beaches, rivers and streams. While Malaysia has amazing beaches on their east coast, most of the west coast beaches lining the Straights of Malacca are polluted and dirty. You'll rarely find any locals swimming in these waters or the inland rivers. Then there are certain experiences in the U.S. that I felt would be better for my son to grow up around, like the zoos. The few zoos I've been to in Malaysia were sad and poorly maintained. Then there are the many other beautiful and amazing national parks and forests that I remember visiting as a child, like the Grand Canyon, Yosemite and Yellowstone national parks. We have things in the U.S. like Niagara Falls, The Smokey and Rocky Mountains, all of which are wonderful sites for kids to go visit. Not to say that Malaysia doesn't have its share of beautiful places to visit. But in the U.S. all these parks and places are set up to better handle visitors and provide better transport systems that make access to them more conducive, especially if trying to take a small child with you.

Here again, all of my arguments have a common theme. These are all aspects of American life that are made possible by functioning government and collective tax dollars. Superior public education, sidewalks, local and national public parks are all possible due to collective tax dollars. Then there are government regulations that help keep our beaches and waterways clean and safe to swim in. Our zoos are heavily funded and subsidized with public money as well.

I don't mean to beat up on Malaysia as if it is some horrible place to live. It's not. The lack of infrastructure that I experienced when I first visited in 2004 has drastically improved and changed quickly over the past 8 years. Back in 1991, Malaysia's Prime Minister at the time, Mahathir Bin Mohammad, announced a bold government plan. His goal was to bring Malaysia up to full developed nation status within 30 years come 2020, and his plan has been working quite well.

While I've complained a lot about life in Malaysia, over the past eight years since my first visit, significant improvements have been made. Eight years ago the intercity bus system was atrocious. Everyday in the newspaper were stories of bus crashes on the highways resulting in hundreds of deaths per year. This was due to old buses, bad highways and tired, overworked drivers. Then the government stepped in. New buses were bought. The highways improved with more highway lighting, guardrails, reflectors and reflective paint. Stricter testing and training were imposed on bus drivers as well as limits on the amount of hours they are allowed to drive. Now the intercity buses are great to ride on and the system functions well.

Like most Asian cities there has been horrible smog problems. Kuala Lumpur wasn't as bad as cities like Bangkok and Beijing, but in 2004 I still noticed slightly brown skies and could smell the smog. Since then all taxicabs were retrofitted to run off of natural gas. Other government controls have been placed on industrial polluters and the result has been much clearer skies in the city.

Ipoh is the second largest city in Malaysia, about 200km North of Kuala Lumpur. It is the town we moved to in 2006. Although it has an airport, all commercial flights stopped operating there for years, due to a badly maintained runway that no one wanted to fix. Years later the government has fixed the runway and commercial airlines are starting to operate out of Ipoh again. Soon more short haul flights will be available, helping to make access to other beaches and points of interests in the country much more convenient. New and faster trains have been built, also making it easier to travel around the country. Oh, also the electricity and water services aren't interrupted anymore like they used to be.

While I believe the education system is still not up to par in Malaysia, the government has increased its budget for education to 23% of all government spending. In the U.S. we barely spend 4% of our budget on education.

One more area to address is that of improved

healthcare services. With globalization you can buy most anything in Malaysia. This includes the latest medical technologies, medicines and procedures. Over the past few years Malaysia has gained more highly trained doctors and hospital facilities have improved greatly. Malaysia has a universal healthcare system as well as private doctors and facilities. While private services cost more and are of better quality, the expense for private care is still relatively low because of competition with the free government health system.

With all these government policies and spending on infrastructure, Malaysia is well on its way to becoming a fully self-sustaining, industrialized, developed nation.

Over the past 20 years the Malaysian government has increased spending on infrastructure and education. It has expanded its power of using government regulations and government market controls. So, if Mitt Romney and all his Republican constituents are correct in their philosophies, then shouldn't we assume that the Malaysian economy was plagued with slow economic growth and high unemployment due to all these increases in "big" government spending and government interference?

Well, actually…..Malaysia's economy grew an average of 7.2% per year throughout the 1990s, twice as much as that of the U.S. economy. In the 2000s, Malaysia's average GDP growth rate was 5.4%, again doubling the U.S. average of only 2% per year from 2000-2010. Also, Malaysia's unemployment rate has remained below 3.5% over the past 20 years, with the exception of the Great Recession when unemployment peaked at 4.1% in 2008. That's half of America's unemployment rate.[lxii]

I would like to sincerely thank and congratulate the Malaysian government for disproving the American Republican theory that increased government spending and regulation leads to slow growth and a stifling of the economy.

Conclusions

We've started our discussion by looking at the purpose of our government. Our founding fathers intended the United States government to protect Freedom and ensure the General Welfare. The two ideas of Individual Freedom and the General Welfare come into conflict with each other in many instances. Things that promote Individual Freedom can go against acting for the Common Good. Placing too much emphasis on promoting the General Welfare can hamper people's Individual Freedoms. Therefore we must strike a balance between these two ideas.

Extremism, placing too much emphasis on one idea or the other upsets this balance. Extreme politicians use tactics in order to sway our opinions one direction or the other, using generalizations to support one theory over another. But one theory alone cannot be used as a way to solve problems without creating further issues in their wake.

We have also looked into what helps to sustain our economy and that is a prospering middle class. As the middle class sinks so does our economy and our country as a whole. We have also shown that it is a fair and progressive tax system that helps to sustain the middle class, which helps to sustain the whole economy. Higher taxes imposed on the wealthy is not meant to punish the rich. A progressive tax system is there to help balance and stabilize a capitalistic system, that when left unchecked leads to a growing gap in wealth disparity. A growing gap in wealth disparity cannot support a healthy economy for long.

We love capitalism and the freedom of the markets. Encouraging people to do better using the profit motive is a powerful force for growth and innovation. Capitalism in America has helped us become the economic powerhouse that we are.

However, we must recognize and remember that our success cannot be solely attributed to our use of capitalism. There is another half to our equation for prosperity and that is smart governance. Through public funding in the form of taxes, we have been able to create a system with

133

infrastructure that helps to support and promote business. America as a collective people have accomplished many grand projects and innovations through the use of our tax dollars, which went to benefit us all as well as private industries.

We are not saying people can't be wealthy. We are not suggesting people shouldn't be free to do well or fail. All we are asking is that those who have done well should have a responsibility; to help support and promote the society that enabled them to become who and what they are. We all still need schools, infrastructure and security. Due to our expanded gap between the rich and poor a majority of Americans can't afford it right now, but the wealthy few can.

The conservative motive or modus operandi has been to bankrupt the treasury through large tax breaks and expensive government contracts, mostly to defense spending. After bankrupting the treasury, the GOP then claims the country is broke. They say that since the government is broke we therefore need to cut spending starting with entitlements, those programs that are giveaways to the most needy. Indeed the United States Treasury is broke, but the country as a whole is not broke. There is plenty of money in the U.S. As a whole country we are still the richest nation on earth. However, a large percentage of our wealth is controlled by only a few of our citizens who purposefully keep money outside the U.S. in order to avoid paying taxes. Claiming the country is broke has been the conservative motive for decades. They claim this in order to shrink government and to pay less in taxes. I don't want a socialist state, nor do I want to carry and pay for those who are lazy. We don't need more government, and we don't need less government, we need SMART government.

We want freedom, freedom to work, freedom to choose, freedom to live. We all want to have the same opportunity but understand we may not all have the same outcome. If you have had that opportunity, now is the time to make sure future generations have the same opportunity as well.

Notes and References

Author's Note on Sources:

This book is an expression of my own overall ideas and opinions based on factual occurrences. I recognize my beliefs and ideas have been formulated and influenced over the years by reading countless book and articles. They are also the product of watching numerous newscasts, interviews and debates on TV. It would be nearly impossible to cite all those sources in this book. However, below is a list of books I offer as Suggested Reading. These books I have chosen were a great source of influence and inspiration for me. There are a few instances throughout this book where I am able to directly reference a specific thought or idea to these other authors. While many of the ideas I have expressed here may not have a specific reference they are still congruent with many of the common themes written in these other books. I would hope that if you enjoyed reading this book that you may further your knowledge of the issues by reading more from these suggested authors.

Many facts and figures used in this book are assumed to be common knowledge. There are many uses of numbers and facts that are widely accepted, reported by multiple sources that can be easily found by anyone. I did not see a need to cite sources for these common facts and figures. Instead I have chosen to save citing references for times when I've used specific quotes, diagrams and facts or figures that may not have been widely reported. I also give specific references for all figures that were used in tables and calculations.

Suggested Further Reading

- Sinclair, Upton. *The Jungle*. New York: Jabber & Company, 1906.   Print
- Friedman, Thomas, and Michael Mandelbaum. *That Used To Be Us*. Farrar, Straus & Giroux, 2011. Print
- Gladwell, Malcolm. *Outliers*. :Little, Brown &

135

Company, 2011. Print
- Chang, Ha-Joon. *23 Things They Don't Tell You About Capitalism*. :Bloomsbury USA. 2011. Print
- Klein, Naomi. *The Shock Doctrine The Rise of Disaster Capitalism*. :Picador, 2008. Print
- Friedman, Thomas. *Hot, Flat, and Crowded*. :Picador, 2009. Print
- Peterson, Peter G. *Running on Empty: How the Democratic and Republican Parties are Bankrupting Our Future and What Americans Can Do About It*. Farrar, Straus and Giroux. July 2004. Print

References

[i] The Constitution (US 1976)

[ii] Saad, Lydia. "Conservatives Maintain Edge as Top Ideological Group." *Gallup Politics*, Oct. 2009. Web

[iii] *CIA World Factbook*. 2009. Web
https://www.cia.gov/library/publications/the-world-factbook/rankorder/2172rank.html

[iv] "Gini Coefficient." *Wikipedia*. 2012 Web

[v] Klein, Naomi. *The Shock Doctrine The Rise of Disaster Capitalism*. :Picador, 2008. Print

[vi] Jarvis, John. "Economics prof provides insights on Arab Spring." The Marion Star. Oct 11, 2011. Web.

[vii] Gastner, Michael., Cosma Shalizi and Mark Newman. "Maps and Cartograms of the 2004 Presidential Election Results." University of Michigan, 2004. Web

[viii] Compiled interviews, *Buffettfaq.com* 2005. Web

[ix] McAuliff, Michael. "Paul Ryan Budget: House Passes Bill To Spare Defense, Cut Food Aid, Health Care" The Huffington Post. May 2012. Web

[x] Evers, Derek. "The Clear Channel Philosophy Lives On, Live Nation And Ticketmaster To Merge?" The Tripwire.com/ Feb. 4, 2009. Web

[xi] "2 Pa. Judges Admit Jailing Kids for Cash." CBS News, May 2009. Web

[xii] "GDP Per Capita" source Worldbank.org. Web. "HMI" source census.gov. Web

[xiii] "Federal Individual Income Tax Rates History." Taxfoundation.org Web

[xiv] "Receipts by Source 1934-2015." Office of Management and Budget, Budget of the US Government FY 2011, Historical Tables, Table 2.1. www.gpoaccess.gov Web

[xv] Leber, Rebecca. "Exxon Mobil's Tax Rate Drops To 13 Percent." Think Progress. March, 2012. Web

[xvi] Duhigg, Charles. and David Kocieniewski. "How Apple Sidesteps Billions in Taxes." New York Times. April, 2012. Web

[xvii] Friedman, Thomas, and Michael Mandelbaum. *That Used To Be Us*. Farrar, Straus & Giroux, 2011. Print

xviii Budget of the U.S. Governmnet. Fiscal Year 2010. Historical Tables: Table 2.1

xix Tax Policy Center. "State and Local Government Finance Data Query System." 2012. Web

xx Lillis, Mike. "Boehner says Obama is inciting 'class warfare'." Thehill.com. Nov. 2011. Web

xxi "Federal Individual Income Tax Rates History." Taxfoundation.org Web

xxii Logan, David S. "Summary of Latest Federal Individual Income Tax Data." The Tax Foundation. Oct. 2011. Web

xxiii Zweifel, Dave. "There Is Class War, and Rich Are Winning". CommonDreams.org. Oct. 2010 Web

xxiv Greenstone, Michael and Adam Looney. "The Great Recession May be Over, Nut American Families are Working Harder Than Ever." The Hamilton Project's Jobs Blog. 12 of 24. Bookings Institute. July, 2011. Web

xxv "United States Housing Prices." Jparsons.net/housingbubble. Web

xxvi "Raise the Minimum Wage." The Editors of Bloomberg News. Boomberg.com. April 2012. Web

xxvii U.S. Census Bureau, Current Population Survey, 1988 to 2011 Annual Social and Economic Supplements. June 2012. Web

xxviii Cornelius, Tamarine. "Wisconsin Budget Project". Wisconsinbudgetproject.org. March 2011. Web

xxix "Labor Union Report: June 2012" LaborUnionReport.com June 2012. Web

xxx Chait, Robin. "Removing Chronically Ineffective Teachers." Center For American Progress. March 2010. Web

xxxi "Current List of Taxpayer Protection Pledge Signers for the 112 Congress." Americans For Tax Reform. Nov 2010. Web

xxxii Silver, Nate. "Moderate Republicans Fall Away in the Senate." The New York Times. May, 2012. Web

xxxiii Stockman, Farah. "Top Iraq contractor skirts US taxes offshore." The Boston Globe. March, 2008. Web

xxxiv Office Of Management and Budget. Historical Tables. Table 7.1 "Federal Debt at the end of the year 1940-2017". Web

xxxv Buffett, Warren. "Stop Coddling the Super-Rich" The New York Times. Aug. 2011. Web

xxxvi Trotta, Daniel. "Cost of War at least 3.7 trillion and counting." Reuters. New York. June 2011. Web

xxxvii Worth, Jim. "War and Taxes." The Blog. Huffington Post. July 2011. Web.

xxxviii Walsh, Deirdre. "House Democrats: No dice on Medicare, Social Security Cuts." CNN. July 2011. Web

xxxix Carpenter II, Dick M., Ph.D., Lisa Knepper, Angela Erickson and John Ross. "License To Work. A National Study of Burdens from Occupational Licensing." Institute for Justice. May 2012. Web

xl Lowrey, Annie. "For Two Economists, the Buffett Rule Is Just a Start." The New York Times. April, 2012. Web

xli Memoli, Michael. "Mitch McConnell's remarks on 2012 draw White House ire." Tribune Washington Bureau. The LA Times. Oct. 27, 2010. Web

xlii "President Reagan did it (raised the debt ceiling) 18 times. George W. Bush did it seven times." www.politifact.com. Web xliii Fidler, Stephen. "Firms Cash Holding Stunts Europe". Wall Street Journal. March 22, 2012. Web.

xliv Johnston, David Cay. "Idle cash piles up: David Cay Johnston." Reuters. July 16, 2012. Web

xlv U.S. Budget for Fiscal Year 2013 Historical Tables. Office of Management and Budget.

xlvi Fidler, Stephen. "Firms Cash Holding Stunts Europe". Wall Street Journal. March 22, 2012. Web.

xlvii U.S. Small Business Administration. www.sba.gov

xlviii Solman, Paul. "Taxes: How high is too high?". PBS reporting series, "Making Sen$e of financial new". Jan 11, 2012. Web.

xlix "Comparing Countries' and Economies' Performance" PISA database. 2009. OECD.org Web

l Johnson, Nicholas. Phil Oliff and Erica Williams. "At Least 46 States Have Imposed Cuts That Hurt Vulnerable Residents and the Economy". Center on Budget and Policy Priorities. Feb 9, 2011. Web

li Crooks, Ed. "German Giant Say US Workers Lack Skills." Financial Times. June 2011 Web

lii "Historical Tables: Budget of the U.S. Government". Office of Management and Budget. Fiscal Year 2011

liii "A Summary Of The 2012 Annual Reports". Social Security and Medicare Boards of Trustees. U.S. Social Security Administration. June 2012. Web

liv Lutz, Ashley. "These 6 Corporations Control 90% Of The Media In America." The Business Insider. June 2012. Web

lv "GDP Growth rates, List by Country." Tradingeconomics.com 2012. Web

lvi Krugman, Paul. "Europe's austerity measures not working, little prospect of a course change." The New York Times. The Economic Times. April 27, 2012. Web

lvii "CNN Poll: 7 out of 10 support 'Buffett Rule'. CNN. April 16, 2012. Web

lviii "Nasa Spinoffs." Spinoff.nasa.gov/ web

lix "Historical Tables, Budget of the U.S. Government." Office of Management and Budget. 2011 Web

lx Simon, Stephanie. "Police, Fire Departments Face Budget Axe." The Wall Street Journal. Feb. 12, 2010. Web.

lxi McMichael, William H. "Families complain of mold at Navy housing." The Navy Times. Dec. 2011. Web

lxii tradingeconomics.com. Database. 2012. Web

A Few Additional Rants

1. <u>Entitlements such as Social Security are……</u>   Let's get one thing straight here. Social Security is not an entitlement program like welfare or food stamps. We've paid into it directly. Social Security is not a free give-away. It is a government required retirement savings that we pay into. What we get out of it is based on what we've paid into the system. The problem with Social Security is that it was set up on a system where the money that goes into it from today's workers is what pays for today's retirees. Which means we now have an issue where more retirees are being paid out than the system has workers putting in.   So there are problems with Social Security but it is certainly not to be classified as a give away entitlement as other programs are. Everyone who receives Social Security paid for it.

2. <u>"I love America", "I believe in America"</u>: Every time we hear a candidate running for office say one of these phrases it can be a great rallying and morale boaster. What is really being attempted every time a politician says, "I believe in America", is to make you think that the "other guy", his opponent doesn't love America. If we are to have any kind of civil, decent political discussions and work together to find solutions, can we please not say or insinuate that your opponent doesn't love his or her country. Just because we may disagree on issues and policy doesn't mean that we don't all love our county. "We All Love America!"

3. The Tea Party gets their name from the Boston Tea Party of 1773. Their current platform and those of Tea Party candidates elected to Congress, support a platform of no taxes. The purpose of the original Tea Party was to protest the unjust taxation of goods by the British monarch. The slogan for the original Tea Party went "No taxation without representation". It wasn't a protest against <u>all</u> taxes, but was against being taxed by an authoritarian government that the

149

people of the colonies had no say or representation in. I find it rather ignorant to invoke the name of the original Boston Tea Party as if it was a fight against any and all taxes. The slogan again was "No taxation without representation", not simply "No Taxes at all, under any circumstances".

No one is Gonna Take away your Guns!

This has got to be one of the silliest on going debates where extremist paint a picture that is way out of proportion. I can understand the difficulty debating issues concerning sensitive and moral topics such as abortion and immigration, but guns? I don't understand why there is a big debate. Oh yeah... extremists.

While I think my beliefs are very centrist, I'm sure extreme Republicans would consider me a Commie Liberal. And in being a tree hugging liberal, I hate guns. I do not own a gun and hope I never feel the need to own a gun. I would much rather wish that the gun were never invented. Even though I hate guns, I do not wish there to be any law banning them entirely. The second amendment in the Constitution says that we all have the right to bear arms and I am glad this amendment is in the Constitution. Guns do have their rightful place in our society for hunting or self-defense.

Studies show that there are more instances where guns in homes cause accidents then instances where they are used for defense. However, I do like the idea that I am free to own a gun if I were to ever feel the need to have one. Even though we have the right to bear arms, in a civil society there does need to be a regard for safety. There do need to be measures in place that prevent criminals who would use guns for ill purposes from having access to weapons. This to me seems like common sense and most Americans feel the same way.

A Reuters poll in April 2012 and an earlier Gallup poll in 2011 both show that even though 80% of Americans support the right to own a gun, 91% still favor the need for background checks, 75% support limiting automatic weapons sales and 62% favor laws banning guns in certain public places such as churches, workplaces, stores and bars.[*]

We can have a balance of ideas, ensuring everyone's right to bear arms and at the same time protecting individuals in society. Imposing regulations to prevent criminals from obtaining guns doesn't stop responsible, law-abiding citizens from being able to own guns. Any proposed regulation does not mean that liberals want to take away your right to own a gun. We are not asking you to give up your weapons. We are talking about sensible regulations to ensure the safety of society. There are safety regulations for driving on the road. Driving a car can kill people and so we have a whole system set-up to ensure people drive safely... So why can't there be rules for gun ownership? Here are some regulations concerning gun control that an overwhelming majority of Americans favor.

1. *Background checks*
2. *Five day waiting period*
3. *Ban on automatic weapons*
4. *Ban on amour piercing bullets*
5. *Ban on certain places where guns can be carried (schools, bars)*

These are all regulations that a majority of Americans support, none of which impose on or prevent any law-abiding citizen from owning a gun. So why would any law-abiding citizen be against the above listed regulations? Why can't a law-abiding citizen wait five days to get a gun? If it prevents criminals and would be wrongdoers from causing harm to others, what's the problem? Why all the forceful outrage against such policies?

---

[*] [1] Charles, Deborah. "Most Americans back gun lobby, right to use deadly force." Reuters. Washington. April, 2012. Web

The BP Oil Spill

If not the worst, at least one of the worst man-made disasters ever was the recent BP oil spill. It started with an explosion killing 12 people. Then it went on for weeks where millions of barrels of oil leaked from the blown oil well into the ocean. Thousands of fishermen went broke while waiting for these contaminates to be contained and cleaned up. People who lived off of tourism in the region took a big hit as well. I am also sure we will never fully understand the entire impact of this incident on the surrounding ecosystems.

All of this tragedy was brought about because of what boils down to one main reason: Profits! This occurred because safety and precautionary measures cost companies money. As of the time I am writing this, there have been reports of safety violations and protocols that went ignored. Not only that, but in the interest of making more profits, procedures were sped up to unsafe levels and certain protocols were skipped all in the interest of maximizing profits.

I fail to see how anyone can argue that private companies will regulate themselves and do what is best for society as a whole. Even the response and clean-up effort by BP was calculated and analyzed to minimize cost, increasing maximum perceived response for PR reasons. None of BP's response effort was done in the interests of the community as a whole. The government had to order BP to stop using harmful oil dispersants, which were not approved by the EPA. These dispersants were only used because they were cheaper and would "disperse" the oil, breaking it up, but it was still there in the water, just in smaller particles that you could no longer see.

Again I fail to see where anything BP has done was in the interest of society or the people. The government even had to freeze 20 Billion of BP's assets to ensure that those families affected by the spill would be compensated and could still afford their homes.

There are those who say it was the MMS's (Mineral Management Service) responsibility to oversee BP. They blame the MMS for being corrupt and it is because that government is corrupt which has led us to this.

152

Yes, people can become corrupted. But if BP were to have done what's right, safe and required on their own in the first place, they wouldn't have to bribe and schmooze the government officials who were supposed to oversee their safety measures.

Bribing is illegal for a reason. Those who offered and those who accept bribes should be in jail. This is a perfect example of how you need accountability for government to work. If there is accountability and systems that make sure our elected officials do the job that they are supposed to be doing, maybe this whole thing would never of happened.

At least there are many instances where government regulations do protect people. Normally when we have accidents such as the BP oil spill or coal mine explosions we often find that government regulations were not followed, ignored and over looked. To say that industry can and should regulate itself; there is no proof that this hands off approach works. There is nothing that says private industry is interested in protecting people and society. However, there are tons of examples where government regulation protects and saves lives. We can't count how many potential accidents have been avoided but we can count the number of accidents that occurred due to industry ignoring government safety regulations. These regulations are meant to protect the public even though they may cut into profits. Of course if a regulation doesn't cost the company anything then they have no problem adhering.

Health Care Law: Mandate? Or Tax Deduction?

The recent highly contested healthcare law, more specifically the portion of the law considered the "mandate" is currently being deliberated in the Supreme Court. The Patient Protection and Affordable Healthcare Act was passed by Congress and signed by President Obama in March of 2010. Part of the idea behind this bill is to lower healthcare and insurance costs by having everyone in the country pay into the healthcare market. While the law expands coverage requirements for insurance companies, it also attempts to help everyone gain health insurance by offering certain tax credits and helps to pay a percentage of people's premiums, depending on your level of income. The part of the law that is considered the "mandate" levies a tax penalty of $695 annually on those people who do not purchase health insurance. This penalty is reduced further depending on income level.

While we may debate the potential benefits, outcomes and effects that this new law could have on our nation's healthcare system, the question being deliberated today in the Supreme Court is the constitutionality of the law, especially the "mandate" portion that will require all Americans to acquire health insurance or face a tax penalty.

First, what makes it a "mandate" and how is it enforced? The answer is through the tax code. Those who don't purchase health insurance will face an added tax penalty. While no one certainly likes the idea of a penalty, what is a penalty for one person could be considered a tax deduction for others.

One question is; "Does Congress have the right to impose a tax in order to steer the healthcare market?" My question is; "How would this be any different from the hundreds of other tax deductions or penalties which the current tax code imposes?"

Since as long as anyone who is alive can remember, Congress has always used the tax code to try and encourage certain behaviors among our citizens. For example, the Mortgage Interest Deduction rewards those who own homes. No one calls it a "mandate" saying that you must own a home and pay interest on an assumed mortgage or face a penalty. But isn't it the same thing? A tax deduction that awards one behavior is a penalty for those who don't follow the same behavior. The idea behind the Home Mortgage Interest Deduction is to encourage people to buy their own homes. People purchasing homes and paying interest on loans, helps to move the economy. In this example the same net goal could be achieved by lowering overall tax rates and instead of a deduction, impose a tax "penalty" on those who don't pay interest on a home loan.

The same reasoning could stand in reverse for the healthcare law. Instead of calling this healthcare requirement a "Mandate" where failure would result in a "Penalty", Congress could have done the opposite. In the interest of having the same net outcome, instead of making a tax penalty, they could have raised the overall tax rates and given a tax deduction to those who did purchase health insurance. If this was the route taken would we still be having a debate about the legality of a "Mandate"?

Another example where the government uses the tax code to encourage a certain behavior is in the area of retirement savings. We want people to save money on their own for retirement. And so the government offers many avenues in which people can save and earn interest on those savings tax-free, through IRAs or 401Ks. While there are these tax savings, the government also imposes a "tax penalty" on your savings if you take the money out of these tax-free accounts too early. All of this is done to encourage people to save for retirement and keep the money in savings for retirement. It is still your money and depending what you do with it, determines if you receive a tax deduction or a tax penalty.

The avenues that the government uses to encourage retirement savings are the same that Congress has decided to use in order to encourage people to buy health insurance. It is still your money and you have the right to choose what you want to do. Those that decide to buy health insurance receive a tax deduction and those that don't, receive a tax penalty. How is this health care law, which uses the tax code to steer behavior any different from all the other tax deductions and penalties that litter our tax code?

My greater concern over the outcome in the Supreme Court is that if they strike down the mandate portion of the law on the basis that Congress doesn't have a right to regulate commerce by imposing tax penalties, then what happens to all the other instances where Congress has done just that by offering deductions. If a tax penalty were deemed unconstitutional, then wouldn't tax deductions, which Congress uses as a tool to achieve the same kind of policy goals be in danger as well?

If the law is struck down on these grounds it could have much further implications than originally intended by those who opposed the law for other reasons.

Acknowledgements

I would like to thank all my friends and family for their continued support. I would especially like to thank my sister Adeena Mignogna, first for helping me to edit this book. I also appreciated her playing the part of devil's advocate, helping me to form more solid arguments. My sister also served as a source of inspiration for me, having self-published two books on her own. And thanks again Adeena for all your continued advice and for helping me to go through the process.

I also need to thank my Dad, Raymond Mignogna for whom without, this book wouldn't have been possible. When this project was in its infancy, my father served as a great sounding board. Many of our conversations involved bouncing ideas back and forth. As a professor of mathematics and statistics, my father was also a great resource, helping me to check my calculations and the reasoning behind them, which were presented in this book.

I would like to thank Lauren Ackert for her added input and corrections. And thanks to thank Charity Lomax for letting me use the picture on the back cover.

This book has been a side project of mine for the past two years. Come early 2012, I wanted to set myself a goal to finally finish. In trying to reach my goal, most of my time off on the road this year has been spent working on this book in the back of the bus. Therefore, I need to thank Dustin Ponscheck for picking up my slack, and to all my other touring cohorts for their continued support and input.

I would like to give a big thanks to all my friends who have engaged in political conversations with me, again helping to better formulate the ideas written in this book. And although this may sound strange, I would like to thank my friends on Facebook, who have put up with my political rants and postings, offering comments and rebuttals of their own.

Finally, I would like to thank all of you who have supported and bought this book, taking the time to read my ideas. I hope you will all be able to take an active roll by further engaging with your peers and discussing in a reasonable, balanced fashion; that we may all come to some consensus.

About the Author

Lawrence Mignogna is a separated father of one, coming from a very modest background and family in New York. He does not posses an advanced degree in anything, having left college after 3 years when offered a job to tour with the Dixie Chicks as they first started out. Lawrence was going to Middle Tennessee State University for Recording Arts and Communications, while working as a live sound engineer and concert promoter in college. Upon being offered his first "real" gig with the Dixi Chicks, he decided to leave college and his bachelor's degree, in exchange for a degree in life.

Working as a live concert sound engineer for the past 15 years, Lawrence has traveled extensively to over 250 cities in over 60 countries around the world. Most of this travel was due to touring with musical artists such as Alicia Keys, Eagles, Britney Spears and Paul Simon to name a few. He has spent some days eating in makeshift restaurants, made out of sea-containers in the slums of Haiti and South Africa, while other days dinning in the finest restaurants, atop the finest hotels in Tokyo, Dubai and New York.

Throughout his career Lawrence has had the privilege to work with people of all different backgrounds from every culture and walk of life. Part of his job involved loading freight onto airplanes with a bunch of Chinese laborers in Beijing, or working with Alabama prisoners who are sometimes used as labor to help set-up concerts in Mobile. Lawrence has also been involved in numerous high-profile events attended by some of the world's top dignitaries.

"One day I could have dinner with a Saudi in Egypt, then the next fly to Norman Lear's private birthday party, in Majorca Spain, on his private jet. Other days I may be walking through cow shit at the Texas state fair, eating fried Hershey bars, after which I have to get showered-up and be on a plane to NY to work on a performance at an awards dinner for the Clinton Global Initiative (talk about a meeting of the minds)."

Lawrence mainly grew up in Commack, New York, on Long Island. Went to high school in Southern Maryland. Lived 8 years in Nashville, TN attending college and the early part of his career. Moved overseas to Malaysia, in Southeast Asia where he lived with his wife and son for 6 years, until recently moving back to Nashville, where he now calls home.